37282

CHE

D0527757

1924471.

Richard Cheetham began his working life in 1978 as a teacher of physics in both the state and private sectors. He was ordained into the Church of England in 1987 and became an assistant curate in Newcastle upon Tyne. While there, as well as leading assemblies in the local primary school, he worked with the staff exploring the issues raised for collective worship by the 1988 Education Reform Act. From 1990 to 1999 he served as a vicar (and latterly as rural dean) in Luton. Among his other responsibilities there he was a member of the inaugural Luton Standing Advisory Committee on Religious Education. In 1999 he became Archdeacon of St Albans, and in 2002 he was consecrated as Area Bishop of Kingston in the Diocese of Southwark, where he also chairs the Board of Education which oversees the work of over a hundred church primary and secondary schools. His research interests centre on the understandings of religious belief in contemporary Britain, and in October 1999 he was awarded a PhD by the University of London for his research into collective worship in schools.

UNIVERSITY OF WALES, NEWPORT

LIBRARY
AND
INFORMATION
SERVICES
CAERLEON

COLLECTIVE WORSHIP

Issues and Opportunities

Richard Cheetham

UNIVERSITY OF WALES, NEWPORT
LIBRARY
AND
INFORMATION
SERVICES
CAERLEON

SPCK

First published in Great Britain in 2004 by
Society for Promoting Christian Knowledge
Holy Trinity Church
Marylebone Road
London NW1 4DU

Copyright © Richard Cheetham 2004

All rights reserved. No part of this book may be reproduced or
transmitted in any form or by any means, electronic or mechanical,
including photocopying, recording, or by any information storage and
retrieval system, without permission in writing from the publisher.

SPCK does not necessarily endorse the individual views
contained in its publications.

British Library Cataloguing-in-Publication Data
A catalogue record for this book is available from the British Library

ISBN 0–281–05586–6

1 3 5 7 9 10 8 6 4 2

Typeset by Land & Unwin (Data Sciences), Northampton
Printed in Great Britain by Ashford Colour Press

For Felicity

without whose love and companionship
neither this book nor many other things
would have been accomplished

Contents

Acknowledgements

A large number of people have been involved in various ways with the production of this book. I first became aware of the importance and potential of collective worship as a window into contemporary understandings of religious belief, especially in public life, through my conversations with the staff of Stocksfield Avenue Primary School in Fenham, Newcastle upon Tyne. This interest soon developed into a doctoral research programme. During that process I was indebted to the many teachers who provided helpful and thoughtful interviews on the issues despite the other heavy demands upon them which were made by their professional lives.

Their reflections were intertwined with those from my supervisors at King's College, London, who provided invaluable and stimulating guidance. My main supervisor, Professor Peter Clarke, gave penetrating and critical comment at crucial moments, and I am also indebted to Mrs Linda Edwards, Dr Andy Wright, and Dr Diane Reay.

I was greatly helped in the completion of my thesis both by the lively interest of the Rt Revd Christopher Herbert, Bishop of St Albans, and by the ambience and community of Westminster College, Cambridge, where I completed most of the writing during a sabbatical in 1998.

Since the completion of the thesis I have been particularly concerned to try to communicate some of the ideas to a wider audience. I have been encouraged in the writing of articles for professional journals by Professor Bob Jackson of Warwick University, who is Editor-in-Chief of the British Journal of Religious Education. Most recently my publishers, SPCK, have given helpful guidance and comment on the production of this book, and I am indebted to Joanna Moriarty, Louise Clairmonte,

Christopher Pipe and especially to Gordon Lamont who has made some useful and penetrating comments. I have also been helped considerably by the advice of those who read some of the draft chapters, and in particular Helen Austin, Jim Jack and Nicola Nathan. In addition to the invaluable support of my wife, Felicity, I have benefited from the continued and thoughtful encouragement and comments of my son, Michael, and my daughter, Sarah.

CHAPTER 1

Collective Worship: The Tip of an Iceberg

Help – I've got to lead assembly!

It was Sunday night and the newly promoted Head of Year 9 at [N] Secondary School was faced with taking assembly at 8.50 a.m. on Monday morning. For fifteen minutes she had to provide something that the law called 'collective worship' for over two hundred 13- and 14-year-olds – a tall order. At the last count she reckoned that there were at least eight different faiths represented among the pupils. Of course, those involved had varying degrees of commitment ranging from very devout to nominal, but there was real religious belief and faith there – both in the pupils and her colleagues – and she had no desire to offend or misrepresent anyone's religious sensibility. There was, too, a large amount of agnosticism, scepticism and sheer indifference in the assembled group. When you added in the ever-present adolescence and hormone mix, it all led to something pretty undo-able; or at least so it seemed on Sunday night. She wished she had stuck to her good intentions and prepared much earlier, but it had been a busy weekend and somehow all the time just went. She was feeling distinctly panicky and unprepared. There had been no training whatsoever for the leading of collective worship. It seemed to be assumed that you could 'just do it' if you had survived in teaching sufficiently long to become Head of Year. Just then she had a flash of inspiration. She remembered the Headteacher had said something to her about 'if you are stuck for ideas try the web'. 'Thank God,' she thought, and rapidly went to <www.assemblies.org.uk> for some illumination.

An hour later the survival plan for 8.50 a.m. to 9.05 a.m. on Monday was in place. She would get through. But there was something still gnawing away in her mind. It went deeper than just getting through the next assembly. Now she was confronted with actually having to lead collective worship on a regular basis she was very uneasy about the whole process. The collective bit was no problem – a collection of all sorts of pupils and teachers. The same went for calling it assembly – all that implied was that they were gathering together for something, and it undoubtedly helped to generate their sense of corporate identity as a year group. But it was the worship part that really troubled her. What did it mean for such a diverse group of pupils who, despite the legal right to withdraw, more or less had to be there? Was it right in an educational context, which was supposed to encourage freedom and clarity of thought, to engage in worship, which seemed to prejudge the question of God? How could worship be forced upon people? What was worship anyway? Did it necessarily involve talk of 'veneration paid to a divine being' as she vaguely remembered from a government circular aimed, somewhat unsuccessfully in her case, at demystifying collective worship? The questions just kept on coming. She would get through tomorrow, but the sense of unease went deep.

Just down the road, at the local primary school, a newly qualified teacher – or NQT as they are inelegantly known – was faced with a related set of problems. Unluckily for him it was his class's turn to do the class assembly later in the term. Your go did not come up very often, but he knew he had to start thinking about it soon because a lot of preparation was needed. He, too, had not had much training for leading assemblies, and was feeling distinctly ill at ease with this aspect of his new job, but he was comforted by the thought that it was the class who would do most of the presentation. They had been looking at the topic of water recently and he had the idea of building something around that – a bit on how important clean water is, and how fortunate we are in Britain to have a plentiful and regular supply, and mention of the one billion people in the world who do not have access to clean water. Perhaps he might find a song about water. But what about the religious bit? It was supposed to be worship – whatever that meant in a school setting. If he threw in a vaguely moral or religious song and added a prayer perhaps that would make it qualify as worship? As far as he was concerned the important thing was to reflect and share something of the work the children had been doing – and perhaps give everyone a little pause for thought in a vaguely moral or spiritual kind of way. He did recall that, according to the 1988 Education Reform Act, part of the school's task was to promote the pupils' spiritual and moral development. Perhaps, he wondered, his class assembly might contribute to that grand aim in some small way, but could it really be considered as an act of collective worship?

On the same day a class tutor in another secondary school was musing over the current 'thought for the week' – spring cleaning – which was supposed to provide the basis for a time of reflection in his tutor group at the end of the day. All everyone really wanted to do, including him, was to go home. But the wretched law required that all pupils should participate in a daily act of collective worship. As it was impossible to fit everyone into the main hall, and it would take for ever anyway to gather everyone together, it had been deemed that the only way to satisfy the legal requirement was for the likes of him to go through the fiasco of an enforced time of reflection, worship, call it what you will, during tutor time. It was bad enough having to take the register. When you had to combine that with a deep thought about the meaning of life at 3.20 p.m. it got just a little difficult. When you had to make it into something that could be called worship – well, really!

Current requirements for collective worship – and the ensuing unease

Situations such as these are repeated time and time again up and down the country. Since the 1944 Education Act a daily act of collective worship has been a legal requirement in all state schools. In that legislation it had to be the whole school assembling at the start of the day. Despite the legal right of withdrawal from assembly, this statute was controversial from the beginning, but the rapid changes in British society since the Second World War (especially secularization and immigration) soon brought massive pressures to bear on schools as they tried to keep the law. The typical format of the school assembly changed under the influence of these pressures from a watered-down church service in the 1950s to the whole variety of pick-and-mix cocktails from the 1960s onwards.

The 1988 Education Reform Act (ERA) tried to provide a more realistic legal framework for collective worship. It sought to satisfy the desire to maintain the Christian heritage of Britain by retaining the legal requirement for daily collective worship and specified that it should be 'wholly or mainly of a broadly Christian character'. It also tried to deal with the reality of multicultural Britain by the allowance of 'determinations'. This was a process which allowed schools to ask permission to be released from the requirement that the worship should be largely Christian in character. This permission had to be obtained from the now statutory Standing Advisory Committee for Religious Education (or SACRE) which every Local Education Authority was required to set up. In addition the 1988 Act addressed some of the practical difficulties of assembly by permitting collective worship to take place at other times of day than the morning, and in other groupings than the whole school. Despite these changes there has been substantial continuing unease about the practice of collective worship which goes on day in, day out in every state school in the land.

A stream of Ofsted (Office for Standards in Education) reports on collective worship have shown widespread non-compliance and dissatisfaction with the law. The analysis of the 2001 SACRE reports states that 'the national picture, in which almost all primary schools provide daily acts of collective worship while most secondary schools fail to meet this legal requirement, is confirmed'. The previous year's analysis stated that 'SACREs continue to be concerned by the legal requirements for collective worship'. On 21 April 2004, in a widely reported speech made at the House of Commons, the Chief Inspector of Schools, David Bell, pointed out that over 76 per cent of secondary schools in England break the law by failing to provide a daily act of collective worship. He argued that it would be sensible to replace the daily requirement with a weekly or even a monthly one. These are just the latest comments in a long line. Throughout the period since the 1944 Education Act, and especially since the 1960s, there have been countless calls for debate and discussion concerning collective worship in schools. These show no signs of slackening. Small wonder that teachers and many others are feeling deep unease about the whole activity.

Problems and tensions facing teachers who lead collective worship

Many difficulties confront teachers in their task of leading collective worship. There are at least nine major problems:

1   confusion of purpose in collective worship
2   the relationship between religious education and collective worship
3   the diversity and plural character of the school community and society at large
4   secularization of society; many people have little or no real link with any major faith, and the related privatization of religious belief – i.e. the view that sees someone's religious belief as a private, individual matter of personal opinion
5   the connection between a pupil's individual beliefs (religious or otherwise) and the values and ethos of the school community
6   the link between moral nurture and religious nurture
7   the relationship between open, critical education and more traditional understandings of education which focus on nurture
8   the position and influence of the teacher's own beliefs in the school context
9   the tension between those who emphasize and encourage induction into the 'Christian heritage' of Britain and those who stress the 'multicultural' aspect of society today.

The number and complexity of these problems makes it very clear that collective worship is not a simple issue. In many respects it is like the tip of an iceberg beneath which are all kinds of issues which face not only schools but wider society as well. Most of these questions concern the way in which contemporary society handles matters of religious belief, moral values and spirituality in general. Collective worship, because it requires some treatment of religious belief in the context of the public education system of this country, is a window into these wider themes. In the practice of collective worship teachers are having to face a whole set of problems and dilemmas which are not simply to do with schools and education, but are deeply rooted in the wider cultural context, as we shall see on a deeper examination of these problems.

The first of the difficulties facing teachers is that there is, and has been since the 1870 Education Act, a confusion over the aims of collective worship in state schools. The Churches' Joint Education Policy Committee (CJEPC) statement on collective worship suggested that 'there should be a clearer appreciation of the nature, aims and objectives of worship in a school context' (CJEPC 1995, paragraph 1.2). The document points to some of the problems in doing this when it says that worship in schools is 'distinctive', i.e. *sui generis*, in that it requires an activity labelled 'worship' (which normally carries many assumptions about belief and commitment) to take place in the context of a school (which normally carries many assumptions about an open, critical approach to education). These tensions were elucidated as long ago as 1975 by the educationalist John Hull in his book *School Worship: An Obituary*. The CJEPC statement is typical of many when it tries to resolve these tensions by arguing for an open, educational approach to school worship which allows, but does not presume, any particular response, whilst at the same time building a sense of school ethos and community (CJEPC 1995, section 3).

There are a number of possible aims for collective worship:

- a social aim of building a sense of school community and ethos
- a moral aim of encouraging good behaviour
- an educational aim of increasing children's awareness and understanding of the variety of world-views and thereby increasing their range of possible choices
- a national aim of promoting a sense of national identity and belonging
- a religious aim of nurturing faith.

In practice there is considerable variety of emphasis among these aims, but broadly speaking the first three aims are largely agreed upon and the last two are much more contentious, especially the last.

The second problem for teachers is the supposed link between collective worship and religious education. In the 1970s it was argued that the experience of collective worship provided some of the raw material for the study of religion which occurred in religious education. More recently some have seen collective worship essentially as an opportunity for religious education – making pupils aware of the diversity of religious beliefs. Increasingly, however, the trend is to see them as quite distinct activities.

The diverse and plural character of the school community is the third major difficulty for the teachers. In the years after the Second World War there was an assumption that the country was homogeneously Christian in character, and school worship drew its rationale and content from Christian sources. With the changes of the 1960s (secularization, immigration, etc.) this assumption is no longer valid. Teachers now often face a hetero-geneous, multicultural school community comprising a variety of religious faiths and other views. Even if a particular school is not so heterogeneous, there is a strong awareness that this is a key feature of wider society which cannot be ignored. There are at least two particular dangers for collective worship in this situation. The first is that teachers resort to a shallow and un-critical relativism, which treats all beliefs as equally valid. There is much evidence, as we shall see, to suggest that this is occurring on a wide scale. The second danger is that, in the absence of a predominant faith, the content of the assembly is largely down to the individual teacher's own choice. Although the law requires that the majority of acts of collective worship 'shall be wholly or mainly of a broadly Christian character' [1988 ERA section 7.(1)], in practice this is interpreted in a very general way and the teacher's influence over both the content and the style of an assembly is substantial. Whilst the judgement of any given teacher may be very good in this matter, it does seem to leave too much discretion and power in the hands of teachers in a crucial area of religious, moral and spiritual formation given the legit-imate claims of families, faith communities and others to have some influence over what goes on.

The fourth difficulty teachers face is the effect of secularization and the privatization of belief. Although the sociological debate over the 'secularization thesis' continues to rage, there can be little doubt that the overt influence of organized religions over many areas of public life has diminished significantly when compared with previous eras of British history (see Wilson 1966, p. 11; Callum 2001). Education is an obvious example: prior to the nineteenth century the Church was responsible for most of the educational provision in this country; now it is the State. For many people religious belief is, at most, marginal to their lives, and the institutional churches and other mainstream religions largely irrelevant. Given this current reality should an act of worship still be mandatory in state schools? One of the consequences of this marginalization of religious belief is that religious belief is often considered to be a private matter for each individual to make a free choice. This is one of the central tenets of liberalism as expressed, for example, in the United Nations Declaration of Human Rights (1948, articles 2, 18, 19, 26). This immediately presents teachers with a clear dilemma: they are being asked to conduct a semi-public act of worship in a state-funded school with a group of pupils who have to be there (for although they do have a right of withdrawal this is rarely exercised) in an area which is a matter of private, individual choice.

The fifth difficulty facing teachers concerns the connection between individual beliefs and school ethos. They are required to do all they can to assist pupils to develop their own individual beliefs and values, whilst at the same time having to 'promote a common ethos and shared values' according to the government circular which attempts to explain how the primary legislation (i.e. the 1988 Education Reform Act) is to be interpreted in practice (Department for Education, Circular 1/94, paragraph 50). There is a clear tension between the two. This is further complicated by the family background of the pupils. What is the school to do if there is a clash in values, as has occurred, for example, with many aspects of the Muslim faith (e.g. dress code, separation of the sexes, diet, prayer times)?

A sixth problem concerns the link between moral nurture and religious nurture. There is significant evidence that governments have used religious education and collective worship as a vehicle for the moral nurture of citizens. Historically the Christian faith has been the main tool for this purpose (Copley 1997, p. 24). It can be argued that the 1988 Education Reform Act is an attempt to resuscitate the Christian faith in this respect (although recent initiatives in spiritual, moral, citizenship and values education suggest that there is a need for alternatives). This approach has many difficulties of which I will mention only two. First, the link between moral education and RE is hotly disputed. Many (e.g. the British Humanist Association) would want to argue that moral education can be undertaken perfectly well on a non-religious basis. Second, it is debatable as to whether or not religious nurture of any kind should be undertaken by a state school.

The seventh problem concerns the understanding of education as 'open' and 'critical'. Many (e.g. Hirst 1974) would argue that encouraging an open and critical rationality where all ideas are subject to scrutinization is of the essence of education. Any approach which seems to assume contentious (religious) beliefs as beyond examination is shunned as 'indoctrination'. There is much evidence to suggest that such a view is very widespread amongst teachers.

The eighth difficulty is the place of the teacher's own beliefs. The teachers bring their own 'baggage' to school. As with any other section of the population some of them hold strong religious beliefs and a few are in no doubt that their religion is the 'best' and 'most true', not only for them in a relative and subjective sense, but for all people in an absolute and objective sense. This has to be held in tension with the professional obligations put upon them by the educational context. They are not to exert undue influence on the children to convert them to their way of thinking. Some adopt a stance of presumed neutrality and would not declare their own views, but only say 'Christians believe . . .' or 'Muslims believe . . .'. Others are prepared to say, 'I believe . . .', but making it clear they do not presume that the pupils have to so believe, and being careful not to make invidious comparisons with other competing beliefs.

The final difficulty is the tension between the 'Christian heritage' lobby and the 'multicultural' lobby. Collective worship (and its Christian bias) has strong popular and legal backing from those who stress the 'Christian heritage' of Britain. But there is also a powerful educational philosophy as expressed, for example, in the major government report which looked at how the education system should respond to ethnic diversity (the Swann Report 1985) and strongly emphasized the equal validity of many world-views. Teachers who have to lead collective worship are caught between these lobbies.

It is fairly clear from the above range and depth of issues that in leading collective worship teachers have to tread a very fine line between many competing forces. It is questionable whether it is possible to find a way of doing this which is both widely acceptable and has a firm educational basis.

Teacher survival tactics

It is not surprising given the complexity of the situation that teachers have developed a variety of tactics for dealing with collective worship and some of the tensions described. Here are the main ones.

- Avoidance, especially of areas of potential conflict between beliefs. There is a strong fear of causing unnecessary offence or upset. Teachers also often speak of their lack of detailed knowledge of different religions which makes them hesitant in saying anything about them for fear of getting it wrong.
- Focusing on the moral issues rather than religious beliefs – which could be construed as a version of avoidance.
- Seeing their role as promoting awareness of the diversity of beliefs so that the children could make their own informed judgement at an appropriate stage. Teachers tend to avoid making judgements between belief systems (i.e. reflecting the phenomenological approach to religious education which stresses the neutrality of the teacher in matters of religious belief, at least in the school context).
- Always prefacing comments about religious belief by such remarks as 'Christians believe . . .' etc. – i.e. making it clear that such beliefs are not being presumed upon the whole population.
- Allowing an 'open' response to what is said or done in collective worship – e.g. giving a time for silent reflection rather than saying a prayer at the end of an assembly.
- Looking for common ground between the different beliefs. Underlying this sometimes is the belief that the different religions are different paths seeking the same goal. One teacher has called this 'essential truth'.
- Promoting attitudes of mutual understanding, respect and tolerance for the diversity of beliefs.

Almost all of these, as we shall explore later, involve operating within a liberal paradigm of education, which emphasizes the freedom of the individual to make his or her own choices in matters of religious belief and world-view, and places much less stress on the idea of nurture into any tradition or community with a shared perspective.

Heroic attempts to salvage collective worship

Given the substantial problems, teachers have exercised considerable ingenuity in reshaping collective worship in a manner which faces up to the current realities of the plural nature of society, is educationally acceptable, and at least attempts to fit in with the law.

The main tactic adopted by teachers is to extend, bend and redefine the concept of 'worship', building on the Old English *weorthscipe*, which means 'worthiness' or 'acknowledgement of worth'. Despite the attempt of the government's Circular 1/94 (paragraph 57) to give worship its 'natural and ordinary meaning' as 'concerned with reverence or veneration paid to a divine being or power', most teachers are much more comfortable with the broader and more inclusive notion of 'worth-ship' as commended, for example, by Gent (1989, p. 9) who says, 'The practical consequences of adopting a wide, inclusive concept of collective worship are far-reaching, the touchstone for the use of any particular style or element within school worship being its capacity to engage people in ways appropriate to themselves.' This approach emphasizes the centrality of the individual's own view as to what is considered to be of ultimate worth. It does not presume anything in terms of religious belief in the pupils, although as we shall see later it has important consequences for the implicit understanding of religious belief which is portrayed when collective worship is undertaken in this manner.

Many teachers make morality the centre of their collective worship. This is often done in the belief that there is a widely agreed moral code which it is acceptable to promote amongst all pupils. Other teachers, but far fewer, use the idea of spirituality as a universal, inner experience as a uniting factor in collective worship, and attempt to develop in pupils the capacity for awe, wonder and reflection on the deeper issues of life. Spirituality is seen as an aspect of being human which all people, religious or not, possess. It is primarily inward, personal and experiential, and therefore is not subject to the obvious problems which occur with the variety of conflicting religious beliefs.

Despite these ingenious and heroic attempts to ensure that the practice of collective worship both complies with the law and has genuine integrity for all who participate, there is still a deep and continuing disquiet about what is going on.

Beneath the tip of the collective worship iceberg

Collective worship requires the practice of a quasi-religious act in a public institution. Thus it raises all kinds of questions about the place of religious belief in public life in Britain today. In this sense it is the tip of the iceberg. We can see and observe what is actually going on in collective worship, but underneath the surface, and less observable, are all kinds of profound issues.

- What is the basic purpose of education?
- What impact does the current practice of collective worship have on pupils?
- Where is the boundary between appropriate nurture (of values and attitudes to life) and unacceptable indoctrination?
- What place does religious belief play in the public life of Britain today?
- What form should that take given both the Christian heritage of Britain and its contemporary multifaith character?
- How do we avoid compromising the integrity of people of differing views?
- What form should any public ritual take, especially in the context of a state school? Should it have any religious element, or should it be such that people of many different viewpoints can participate on an equal basis?
- How do we understand and deal with the differing 'truth claims' of religions?
- Are there any common moral values in Britain today? If so, how should they be encouraged, particularly in schools? What is their moral authority?
- Is there a spiritual core to all world-views? Does the notion of spirituality have any content?
- Is there any common understanding of the 'good life' – i.e. the basic view about how human life is best understood and lived?

It is the argument of this book that the reason why it has been so difficult to find a consensus on collective worship is that it embraces all these profound issues. They are all there beneath the tip of the collective worship iceberg. They need to be thoroughly explored in order to find a way forward for collective worship which does not entail the present tensions and dilemmas. The current state of British society is one of huge flux. We are still deeply influenced by our more homogeneous Christian past, but also are coming to terms with and embracing a much more pluri-form and postmodern Britain in which all kinds of viewpoints coexist and are learning how to get along with each other in a way that both celebrates diversity and embraces the need for unity and common purpose.

The importance of 'key locations'

There has been a vast amount of literature on all of these issues. Most of it comes from a theoretical standpoint. However, substantial insights into what people actually believe can be found by looking at certain places or contexts in British society where the issues come above the surface and decisions about how to act have to be taken. I call these contexts 'key locations'. Collective worship in schools is one such key location. An examination of how teachers are actually responding to the demands of this situation tells us much about their underlying beliefs. Put more simply, actions speak louder than words.

There are many such key locations in society. For example:

- civic services
- chaplaincy provision in public institutions such as prisons, hospitals and universities (whether it is Christian, multifaith or a generalized 'spiritual care')
- the practice of the 'occasional offices' of baptisms, weddings, and funerals
- the place of religion in the mass media
- national times of mourning and celebration and how these are marked
- the interrelationship between Church and State.

The real decisions that are taken in such key locations give crucial insights into how our society handles the deeper issues of basic beliefs and values. It is a vital area of research, but surprisingly little empirical work has been done.

This book explores one such key location, collective worship in schools, in the twin beliefs that examining the current practice will yield helpful information on the deeper issues, and that no way forward can be found for collective worship until these deeper issues are brought to the surface. There are many published books and other material which give very helpful ideas for the practical delivery of assemblies. Daily collective worship is a voracious animal; hard-pressed teachers, even the most dedicated and creative, will need a considerable supply of ideas and resources if they are to satisfy the law and deliver a high quality experience for the pupils. However, there is a real dearth of material which looks at the deeper issues raised by the practice of collective worship. In many respects this is surprising, given how contentious an area it is. Most of this work can be found in diverse educational journals and teachers' magazines.

There have been numerous publications in the related areas of spirituality, moral and values education, and citizenship. In some ways these can be seen, at least in part, as attempts to provide a new rationale for collective worship which goes beyond the religious. These ideas seek to embrace people of a wide variety of views in a common and agreed understanding of the central roles of education. Part of the debate over collective worship relates to issues at the very heart of the educational process – namely the basic moral and spiritual values, and the visions of life, which underpin what goes on in schools. These publications give much valuable food for thought, but none of them deals directly with the issue of collective worship.

Another reason for the dearth of books on the theory of collective worship is the surprising lack of research into what is actually going on. The major overview is given by the Qualifications and Curriculum Authority's annual analysis of SACRE reports on *Religious Education and Collective Worship*. However, as the analysis of the 2000 reports says, the main source of information used by SACREs is the Ofsted reports on schools in their area, and the coverage of collective worship in these is 'still uneven'. In the words of one SACRE report, 'judgements on quality were rare'. Another SACRE complained of totally inconsistent judgements made on collective worship in two primary schools, each of which had followed the SACRE guidelines. On a more academic front there has been some quantitative research, notably by Leslie Francis, and a number of MA dissertations, but the overall amount of proper analysis and information is very small.

This current book draws on a substantial recent piece of qualitative doctoral research into collective worship which I undertook in the late 1990s (Cheetham 1999). It was based on a sample of twelve schools in [x] town. It included two infant (5–7-year-olds), five junior (7–11), one primary (5–11), and four secondary (11–16) schools. Two of these were Church schools, one Roman Catholic and one Church of England. The sample made no pretence at being random, but was broadly representative of state education in [x] between the statutory school ages of five and sixteen, including a wide range of ethnic and faith backgrounds amongst the pupils. I sought to elucidate and analyse some of the deeper issues underlying collective worship using in-depth interviews with teachers who led collective worship, together with observation of what actually went on, and analysis of the various documents (school policies, etc.) which surround the practice. In particular, the aim of the research was to produce a critical description and analysis of the understanding of religious belief which underlies the current practice of collective worship. This research brings significant new insights based on empirical evidence rather than presumed theory or anecdote. The research aimed to explore the views and understandings of those most closely responsible for delivering collective worship – i.e. it focused on the teachers who led it. It did not examine the pupils' responses and attitudes. There has been some work in this latter area, but again, it is very small given the scale and complexity of the issues. Such an addition to the research base would be very welcome and an important adjunct to the perspective of this publication.

Who is this book for?

This book is aimed at anyone who is interested in the practice of collective worship and its wider implications including:

- *Teachers*, and especially those with a particular responsibility for collective worship (e.g. headteachers and other teachers in the senior management teams of schools, RE teachers and others). The evidence from my research suggests that those who lead collective worship think deeply about its character and would appreciate a clear account of the issues which are not far from the surface.

- *Trainee teachers.* There is currently no single book dealing with the issues surrounding collective worship which can be recommended to trainee teachers. Collective worship is a whole school issue which is, at present, somewhat neglected in initial and subsequent teacher training. Given the significant role played by collective worship in schools it is essential that teachers understand the deeper questions at the outset of their career.
- *Politicians, civil servants and others involved in local and central government.* Many people have an interest in, or responsibility for, collective worship. These include those from the Department for Education and Skills, the Qualifications and Curriculum Authority, the Office for Standards in Education, local authority Education Committees and Standing Advisory Committees for Religious Education, etc. Everyone involved in these bodies has a responsibility to reflect upon the nature of collective worship and its place, not only in the life of the school, but in terms of its significance for wider society.
- *Parents* concerned for the spiritual and religious upbringing of their children and the appropriate role of state schools need to know what is going on and how they can work in partnership with the school in the nurture and education of their children.
- *School governors* who have the responsibility for approving a school's collective worship policy need to do so with a full understanding of the implications of such policies.
- *People from different faith communities*, including the clergy, interested lay people, those involved in church and other faith schools all need to bring their influence to bear in an informed manner.
- *Those with a general interest in the role of moral and spiritual values, and of religious belief, in contemporary society.* The current practice of collective worship gives important insights into the way in which such issues are handled in contemporary society.

An outline of the book – as a guide to how to make best use of the material

Chapter 2 deals with *the historical background* from the 1870 Education Act onwards, but concentrating on those aspects which are relevant to the current situation. It focuses particularly on the contrast between the assumptions of the 1944 Education Act (that schools helped to promote the ethos of a largely 'Christian' England) and those of the 1988 Education Reform Act (that the multifaith, plural character of England had to be taken much more seriously). It concludes with a description of the characteristics of the current practice of collective worship.

Chapter 3 examines the underlying *sociological issues* including:

- the changing religious and spiritual character of the UK; the transition from modernity to postmodernity (especially the approach of liberalism to religious belief and critiques of that view)
- the desire for unity and common ground both within a school and in wider society (including the place of citizenship in this regard)
- the importance of individual freedom of choice regarding 'lifestyle options'.

Chapter 4 considers the *educational issues* including:

- a discussion of different understandings of the nature of the educational process (traditional, liberal and postmodern views) in relation to religious belief and collective worship
- the implications of these for the handling of collective worship
- the very substantial influence of the individual teacher in moulding and shaping what goes on in collective worship
- the need for a more overt recognition of the underlying philosophy of education of individual schools.

Chapter 5 explores the *ethical questions* including:

- the widespread desire for common shared values (and the basis of any such value system)
- the use of collective worship as a tool for moral education
- how we avoid indoctrination – the inappropriate manipulation of pupils into the values and outlook of their educators

- how we develop, in a plural culture, morally appropriate attitudes towards those with differing views and how we interpret the ideas of tolerance, respect and mutual understanding.

Chapter 6 investigates *theological and philosophical matters* including:

- different understandings of the nature of religious belief (and particularly the question of 'truth claims')
- how religious belief is treated in practice in current collective worship
- the nature of spirituality and its relationship to traditional religious belief in the context of collective worship.

Chapter 7 explores the *different options for the future of collective worship*. This begins with an outline and critique of the current prevailing practice. It then looks at four different possibilities in the light of the issues. These options are:

- the status quo
- removing the current legislation and allowing each school to decide what it wishes to do
- proscribing collective worship altogether in state schools
- replacing the requirement for collective worship with one which legislates for an act of 'collective spirituality or reflection'.

Summary

Collective worship is an important, but deeply problematic and controversial, public issue of widespread significance and interest. Many teachers, such as those mentioned at the beginning of this chapter, are having to deliver assemblies aware that there are serious problems with the basic framework and understanding within which they are required to operate. Collective worship is the tip of an iceberg with many profound issues which affect wider society lurking beneath the surface. It requires clarification of the underlying issues and substantial further debate in order to establish a satisfactory theory and practice for the twenty-first century. This book is a contribution to that debate.

CHAPTER 2

The Historical Background and Current Debate

Introduction

The current arrangements for collective worship are the outcome of a long, slow, and sometimes tortuous evolution. The end product is a practice which is the result of many compromises. Few people are genuinely happy with the existing legislation and it is scarcely a coherent position for the twenty-first century. Recent Ofsted reports on collective worship have shown widespread non-compliance with the legal requirements, especially in secondary schools. Some of these are quite blatant in not intending to do anything about this because they consider the law to be deeply unsatisfactory. Throughout the period since the 1944 Education Act, and especially since the 1960s, there have been countless calls for debate and discussion concerning collective worship in schools. This shows no sign of slackening. This chapter gives an account of how we have arrived at this situation, and highlights the key underlying themes and issues in this extraordinary saga.

Prior to the 1944 Education Act

The nineteenth century saw the establishment of a national system of education that was a partnership between the Church, which hitherto had had enormous control over virtually all education in this country, and the State, whose influence was steadily increasing, especially from the 1870 Education Act onwards. Throughout the nineteenth century both the Church of England and the Nonconformist churches were active in establishing their own schools and there was considerable rivalry between them. In addition, the Roman Catholic Church, having suffered from centuries of tight restriction since the Reformation, was benefiting from significant new legal freedoms and it, too, was seeking to establish its own schools.

Up until 1870 the State had only been involved in the provision of education in a minor way, but that changed substantially with the passing that year of the Elementary Education Act. This established 'board schools' to fill the gaps between the voluntary church schools. As with the subsequent Education Acts (e.g. 1902, 1944, 1988) the religious education sections were only a small part of the whole, but they generated considerable controversy. At this time the problems were mainly concerned with interdenominational rivalry and with the propriety of State financial support for religious instruction and church schools. Two main provisions were made to deal with these issues. First, the famous 'Cowper–Temple clause' stated that 'no religious catechism or religious formulary which is distinctive of any particular denomination' should be taught in the board schools. Religious Instruction (RI) in schools was to be non-denominational, which effectively limited it to the teaching of Bible stories. This immediately indicated that what was going on in the board schools was of a different nature to what went on in the church schools with regard to religion. The State did not care to arbitrate between the various religious views as to their truth and so required a new form of religious instruction, non-denominational, to be created. This unique format of State-school religious education has continued in one form or another ever since. The second provision made by the 1870 Education Act for dealing with the problems raised by RI was a 'conscience clause' which gave parents the right to withdraw their children from RI if they so wished. The State had a duty to protect the freedom of belief of its citizens. Both of these provisions indicated an awareness of the difficulty of providing for worship and religious education in state schools.

During the nineteenth century and well into the twentieth, school worship consisted mainly of daily 'observances' which were catechetical in style – a mixture of RI and worship that focused on reciting, for example, the Lord's Prayer, the Ten Commandments and the Apostles' Creed. In the aftermath of the First World War a significant shift occurred in the approach to school worship. For a period of about forty years schools were largely seen as Christian communities and the task of assemblies was to affirm Christian values and to nurture faith – an implicit assumption was being made about the 'truth' and validity of the Christian faith. A more confessional approach was being adopted which was exemplified by the widely used Cambridgeshire Agreed Syllabus of 1924 which stated that

> All education, rightly conceived, is religious education . . . the crucial question in Religious Education must be, so far as the school is concerned, 'Is the school a Christian community? Does membership of the school give a Christian character?'

Part of the driving force behind this approach was the perceived need for a strong moral and spiritual framework for life after the carnage of the First World War.

The 1944 Education Act

The war-time influence was again a significant factor in the shaping of the religious provisions of the 1944 Education Act. A *Times* leader from the early years of the Second World War commented:

> The truth is [. . .] that education with religion omitted is not really education at all [. . .] It will be of little use to fight, as we are fighting today, for the preservation of Christian principles if Christianity itself is to have no future, or at immense cost to safeguard religion against attack from without if we allow it to be starved by neglect from within . . .   (*The Times*, 13 February 1941)

Similar sentiments were frequently expressed in the parliamentary debates preceding the passing of the 1944 Education Act. It is interesting to note that the *Times* leader used the phrase 'Christian principles', possibly indicating that what was really valued was not Christian doctrine and belief, but Christian morality and behaviour – i.e. taking a pragmatic view of religious belief which stressed the importance of its effects in the believer's life rather than the 'truth' or otherwise of its doctrine.

As with the other Education Acts it needs to be remembered that the education system was undergoing huge changes: in 1944 these included the establishment of the primary, secondary and further education stages, and the important general requirement that local education authorities should 'contribute to the spiritual, moral, mental and physical development of the community' through the provision of efficient education (section 7). The religious education provision was only a small, albeit significant, part. It reflected a balance of interests between Church and State in the system of dual control – a balance which had been steadily shifting in the State's direction since 1870. Section 15 established three categories of voluntary school ('aided', 'controlled', and 'special agreement') with varying degrees of state financial support and church control over their running.

The main elements of the Act with regard to school worship and religious instruction were laid down in section 25, which said that 'the school day in every county school and in every voluntary school shall begin with collective worship on the part of all pupils in attendance', and that 'religious instruction shall be given in every county school and in every voluntary school'. In addition to this basic provision, parents retained the right to withdraw their children from RI and collective worship (section 25), and teachers not to participate. 'Worship' was not defined in the Act, and neither the content nor the form was prescribed other than the requirement that it should be non-denominational (section 27). A clear assumption was that the provision for school worship and RI was part of the Christian education of the nation's children.

This was a new era for educational legislation because, although it only enshrined in law what had been the predominant practice in the vast majority of schools, there had never before been a legal requirement for school worship or RI. Although, at the time, some doubted the wisdom of making school worship compulsory there was very strong public and parliamentary support in favour of the legislation. However, there were some hints that this consensus was not as complete as it might have seemed when the Act was passed. During the course of the debates the phrase 'corporate worship' which had been in the White Paper was replaced by 'collective worship' (1944 Education Act, section 25), indicating a recognition that not all those present at school worship would necessarily be of one mind on Christian belief and that it had to be recognized that each individual would make his or her own response. In addition, in section 7 (see above), the word 'religious', favoured by Archbishop William Temple, was replaced by the vaguer and more general word 'spiritual' suggesting an acknowledgement that the country was not simply homogeneously Christian. The judgement of hindsight has suggested that the Act had sown the seeds of continuing problems. It may have reflected a general consensus in English society in the first half of the twentieth century, but the tumultuous changes which were to occur in the second half of that century meant that the provisions of the Act were problematic almost before the ink was dry.

In the 1950s and into the 1960s the general approach by schools was to try to implement the requirements of the Act, and to do it well – i.e. a largely confessional view was adopted, although underlying tensions were beginning to appear. Assemblies, for the most part, took the form of 'watered-down' church services (e.g. a hymn and Bible reading followed by prayer), and many teachers seemed to regard their task as preparing children for the worship of the Church and nurturing them in the Christian faith, trying to make what they did as relevant as possible to the experience of the children.

The upheaval of the 1960s

By the 1960s many problems were beginning to emerge which had a profound effect on school worship. It is possible to discern at least five major areas of difficulty.

First, immigration was bringing people of other faiths to Britain in large numbers. In many towns and cities it could no longer be assumed that the children in school were from Christian families, however nominal. There were now significant alternatives to Christianity, and each religion made its own truth claims. The comfortable assumptions of the 1944 Act concerning the Christian character of the country could no longer be made so easily. Britain was rapidly becoming a plural, multicultural society.

Second, the process of secularization seemed relentless. There was a continuing, inexorable decline in church attendance including Sunday Schools. The country was not without religious and spiritual beliefs, but those beliefs were becoming more varied and less connected with the institutional churches. In addition, the voices of those of humanist, secularist, atheist or agnostic persuasion were no longer as muted as they had been in the depths of the Second World War.

Third, educational questions were being asked about whether or not children were able to understand the religious concepts implicit in an act of collective worship. The work of Ronald Goldman (1964) on the religious understanding of children at various stages in their development was very influential, although some of his conclusions have been seriously questioned since that time. In addition, Harold Loukes' research had shown that many teenagers had found their lessons on the Bible to be 'childish and irrelevant' (Loukes 1961, p. 150). It had been taught too often without any application to their lives. He advocated the 'problem method' approach which began with a problem or issue that was directly relevant to the teenagers and only then proceeded to the Bible's teaching. The implicit assumption seems to be that the truth of Christian belief and faith is to be found not in dry doctrinal propositions, but in the effects of belief in the life of the believer – i.e. a pragmatic approach to its truth where the central issue is, 'does it work?'

Fourth, some educationalists suggested that there was a tension between the aims of worship and the aims of education: the former assumes belief and commitment, the latter encourages an open and critical stance which scrutinizes belief. In 1970 a major Church of England enquiry into Religious Education (the Durham Report), in reviewing the arguments against school worship, commented, 'School worship presupposes the truth of Christian theological propositions and assumes the validity of the practices of Christian prayer' (Durham Report 1970, p. 132). Such presuppositions were strongly questioned in the 'open' and liberal society which was fast developing in the 1960s and, in particular, it was doubted that worship could be made compulsory as it is, in essence, a freely given response.

Fifth, the 'new' and radical theology of the 1960s (which, in fact, only popularized some of the ideas that had been current in academic theological circles for many years), exemplified by the Bishop of Woolwich's 1963 publication *Honest to God*, had shaken the foundations of much traditional Christian belief. What had previously been thought of as Christian truth now no longer seemed so certain and the 'new theology' seemed to focus on a more immanent understanding of God as 'ultimate concern' or as 'the depth and ground of being'. This redefinition of religion led to a view of religious education as primarily enabling pupils to reflect on their lives and to discover their own deepest concerns and the implications of that for the way they should live.

These problems meant that many people thought school worship could no longer survive in the open, plural society which Britain was becoming. In 1971 the Schools Council's Working Paper No. 36, which had a very substantial effect on the teaching of RE, spoke of 'the absurdity and dishonesty of expecting pupils from a wide variety of backgrounds to participate in something that the majority of their parents have little time for, and which they cannot yet evaluate objectively, however they react now' (Schools Council 1971, p. 97). Although it advocated the advantages of assembly for 'a quiet period in adolescence, the fostering of school spirit, the inculcation of values, the promotion of social awareness, and the civic advantage of having some acquaintance with ritual' (p. 98), it was heavily critical of the formality, dullness and confusion of aim of assembly in a 'multi-religious' situation, and suggested that school worship 'really requires a curriculum development project of its own' (p. 100).

The problems were such that, in 1975, the educationalist John Hull could write a book entitled *School Worship: An Obituary*. The thesis of the book was summarized on the back page as follows: 'Worship in daily assembly is an anachronism, inadequate as worship and ill-related to the needs and concerns of the school and the society in which it is situated.' Hull argued that worship (which assumes belief) and education (which scrutinizes belief) 'can never take place concurrently' (p. 59) and that 'compulsory school worship is the most objectionable example of compulsion which the school offers its pupils' – encouraging both hypocrisy and the compromising of conscience (p. 120). In response to this situation Hull called for a 'radical overhaul'. Hull's stringent and influential critique summed up the views contained in many articles throughout the 1960s in Religious Education journals (especially *Learning for Living*) and elsewhere. The provisions of the Act were clearly not working as intended. Something had to be done.

The response to the problems

One significant response from the churches to the rapidly changing situation was *The Fourth R* – the Durham Report of 1970. This was a major review of Religious Education sponsored by the Church of England's Board of Education and the National Society which recognized, at least in part, many of the above problems facing school worship. The report rejected the view that England was 'a post-Christian, religiously neutral society' and argued that it was more accurate to describe England as 'a post-ecclesiastical society, evincing varying degrees of Christian commitment and association' (para. 307, p. 139). It also recognized the significant difference between school worship and church worship, with the former being more akin to civic services and the like which 'do not presuppose the individual commitment of all those who attend them; they have a symbolic significance, representing society's disposition towards religion' (para. 302, pp. 137–8). The report concluded that

> regular opportunities for school worship should continue to be provided for two principal reasons:
> (a) The experience of worship is a necessary part of religious education.
> (b) School worship is expressive of society's positive disposition towards religion and contributes to the preservation within the school community of those spiritual, personal, and moral values which derive from the Christian tradition.   (para. 308, p. 139)

The issue of the 'truth' of the Christian faith was not dealt with directly, but was never far from the surface. A crude confessional approach was rejected as inappropriate in schools – that was the task of the churches and other similar religious bodies – but the teacher was to press for 'commitment to the religious quest, to that search for meaning, purpose and value which is open to all men' (para. 217, pp. 103–4). The task of school worship as part of RE according to the Durham Report, was the educational one of giving pupils the necessary experience to undertake that quest in an informed manner (para. 117, pp. 60–1). There was clearly a hope that pupils would come to a real Christian faith – and this hope was there not only because the Christian faith was seen as part of the heritage of this country and as helpful in preserving its moral ethos, but also because of the belief that the Christian faith is true (para. 213, pp. 102–3). The bias of the report towards the truth of the Christian faith was shown in three revealing ways. First, the possibility of solely secular or 'shared values' assemblies was rejected on the grounds that such assemblies have 'very clear irreligious implications' and that they might imply erroneously that 'the contemporary debate between the religious and secularist interpretations of life had been settled' (para. 306, p. 138). Second, they did 'not recommend the regular adoption of acts of worship supposedly designed to meet the needs of those of all faiths and of none'. They stated clearly that 'services consisting of hymns of nature, prayers of universal appeal, together with readings from all the religions and philosophies of the world are not, in our view, desirable as regular acts of school worship' (para. 316, p. 141). And third, the report did not really engage with the plural character of British society and the presence of people of other faiths. Concerning assemblies for those areas of the country where there was a substantial immigrant population they only recommended an ad hoc pattern (para. 315, p. 141).

The schools' response to the problems of the 1960s and 1970s suggested that the Durham Report had missed the mark, at least in its assessment of the teachers' attitudes and disposition towards religion and the Christian faith in the life of the school. Several articles in professional journals (especially *Learning for Living* and the *Times Educational Supplement*) in the 1960s and 1970s suggested that during this period there were many calls for a more open approach which recognized that schools were on the frontier in a rapidly changing society that was now much more pluriform in character.

The worship requirements of the 1944 Education Act were largely ignored and assemblies were rapidly becoming general reflections on humanitarian concerns with the focus being immanent rather than transcendent. Increasingly the assumption was that an assembly was made up of all faiths and none, with a great variety of belief and commitment represented. Worship was no longer understood in a purely religious sense (with reference to the transcendent), but was broadened to mean 'worth-ship' – i.e. celebrating and reflecting upon that which was considered to be of ultimate worth and concern. There was a focus on universal ethical truths and moral education because it was assumed that there was common ground in this area between the multiplicity of beliefs. New song books appeared which contained more general and inclusive songs; the same happened with prayer. The early tactics of some London schools in dealing with their new multicultural situation included: revising their hymn books to include more religiously neutral songs; looking for universal ethical truths, using inclusive prayers, encouraging respect for all traditions, learning about each other's faiths and identifying common themes across all religions. In 1969, in a book entitled *Worship in the Secondary School*, Jones argued that the favourable climate to Christian school worship which surrounded the 1944 Education Act was beginning to break down and that more 'ambivalent' assemblies were needed which took into account the 'multi-belief' character of the school (Jones 1969). He characterized such an assembly as 'one that is sufficiently open for the members of a mixed congregation to make a whole range of different responses according to their personal inclinations' (p. 97). It should also explore common values and concerns; understand worship as 'seeing ultimate worth and responding to it' (p. 100); exclude traditional hymn singing and prayers; and allow an open response to what is said (p. 16). A few years later, writing in 1975, John Hull argued in *School Worship: An Obituary* that school worship should be made a far more open experience which can be seen as 'being a threshold for worship'. He said, 'Such assemblies will not seek to secure commitment, nor to profess faith, but to deepen under-standing and to facilitate choice'. So, for example, far greater use was made of stories with moral themes, and there was more emphasis on 'universal' themes such as hope, wonder, wisdom etc. An assembly might seek to explain or describe what a particular religion taught, but make no assumption about whether or not it was in any sense 'true'. In these approaches we can see a powerful trend away from the assumption of the truth of the Christian faith which had undergirded many traditional assemblies and towards a more neutral and non-committal stance.

The emphasis on neutrality towards the truth of different beliefs was strongly reinforced in the phenomenological approach to the teaching of RE which was very influential in the attitude to religion in schools from the 1970s onwards. This approach sought to get away from confessional stances and did not seek to promote any one religious viewpoint, but encouraged pupils to try to understand the 'life-world' of the believer in an empathetic manner. The emphasis was on trying to understand what it meant to practise and believe a particular religious viewpoint rather than evaluating whether or not it was credible or true. There was certainly no attempt to nurture children into a particular faith – Christianity or any other. This approach gave rise to a considerable debate about the place of the teacher's own beliefs in education.

The Schools Council's Working Paper No. 36 (1971) was extremely influential in promoting the phenomenological approach to RE in schools. Underlying its approach, and of particular importance, was the dominance at this time of the liberal model of education, which stems from the Enlightenment. It had at its heart a belief in an overarching, universally agreed form of human reason and 'objective' knowledge, and a strong view of the autonomy and freedom of the individual. The paper argued that, 'Objective teaching seeks to present evidence for beliefs, so that they can be accepted or rejected freely and intelligently' (p. 24). This approach to liberal education was strongly influenced by the views of the educationalist Paul Hirst, who argued in the 1960s and 1970s that education was centrally about 'knowledge' and the critical use of human reason. The problem with RE and religious beliefs was that there were no publicly agreed criteria by which conflicting truth-claims could be settled and, therefore, they are to be seen as 'a matter of personal preference'. This means the school should be 'genuinely uncommitted religiously' (Hirst 1974, pp. 181–2). Hirst's understanding of religious belief seems to underlie the approach taken in Schools Council's Working Paper No. 36. In the discussion of the problems facing teachers who hold Christian beliefs the paper says:

> Education presupposes a common basis of agreement about what constitutes knowledge and what is only opinion. At the present time Christianity, in the view of the majority, falls in the second category. The beliefs of Christians (and those of other faiths and ideologies) can only, in these conditions be presented as 'what some people believe'. . . In brief, Christianity as truth no longer belongs to this common basis of agreement – except within the environment of the

Church; it follows that outside this 'voluntary association'
what Christians believe can only be classified as such, not
as common knowledge shared by all.

(Schools Council 1971, pp. 92–3)

This has been quoted at length because it shows very clearly how
the doctrine of liberal education treated religious belief as private
opinion rather than public knowledge. There is much evidence to
suggest that this view is still paramount among teachers today,
despite the development of a number of significant critiques of
liberal education coming from various different stances – both
religious and non-religious (Cooling 1994; Ashraf 1997; Halstead
and Khan-Cheema 1987; Sarwar 1994; Muslim Education Forum
1997; Usher and Edwards 1994; Polanyi 1958; MacIntyre 1988).
I shall return to various aspects of these critiques later on. The
main points to emphasize at this stage are the dominance of the
liberal view (with its allegedly 'neutral' and 'non-committal'
stance towards religious belief) in the 1960s, 1970s and continuing
to the present, and the fact that this dominance is beginning to
crumble.

The 1980s

Even the changes, described above, in the practice of assemblies
to make them more 'open' were not enough to quell the serious
disquiet concerning collective worship. Evidence given to the
House of Commons Select Committee for Education, Science and
Arts in 1981 included opposition to the collective worship provision coming from two quite different directions – the National
Secular Society (on the grounds of lack of impartiality and
imposed hypocrisy), and the British Evangelical Council (on the
grounds that Christian worship cannot be validly undertaken by
those not of Christian persuasion). The Select Committee also
noted the comment from the Church of England's Board of
Education, 'The Board accepts the difficulty at the present time
of implementing the law relating to a daily act of worship . . .
The problems are immense . . .' The Select Committee's recom-
mendation was that

the Secretary of State should now begin to have discussions
with interested bodies, including the church authorities

about guidance to schools (on the act of school worship). These discussions should include the possibility that legislative changes may be necessary.

Similar views continued to be expressed throughout the 1980s. For example, a report from the National Association of Headteachers, published in 1985, expressed a concern that in many places the requirements of the 1944 Act in relation to morning assembly and the corporate act of worship were 'impossible to implement fully and honestly and properly'. The reason given for this concern was 'the radical changes in the make-up and the mores of society since 1967 and more so since the Education Act of 1944' (National Association of Headteachers 1985, p. 3).

A major government report from 1985 tried to tackle one aspect of these changes – the advent of multiculturalism. The central question of the Swann Report was how the education system should respond to the ethnic diversity of Britain. There was a particular concern about finding ways of tackling under-achievement by many pupils from ethnic minorities. The Swann committee developed the notion of 'Education for All' which reflected the diversity of British society and aimed at developing sensitivity towards the cultures and practices of ethnic minorities and promoting greater understanding and mutual respect between cultures. The report encouraged a positive attitude to plurality and diversity. With regard to religious education the report was 'firmly in favour of the broader phenomenological approach to religious education as the best and indeed the only means of enhancing the understanding of all pupils, from whatever religious background, of the plurality of faiths in contemporary Britain . . .' (p. 474). The Report's view on collective worship was that they did 'not believe that this requirement can continue to be justified with the multiplicity of beliefs and nonbeliefs now present in our society' (p. 497). Swann was very firmly moving away from regarding Christianity as in any way superior to other faiths and from treating British culture as better than other cultures. Within this approach, questions of the truth or otherwise of conflicting religious beliefs were inevitably sidelined in the overwhelming desire to achieve parity of esteem between cultures. Underlying this was the notion that there was a framework under which it is possible to hold all the cultures and beliefs together in a single school: and that framework was provided by the liberal ideal of education, now firmly multicultural in form and with an implicit relativism towards religious belief as the following quotation suggests:

> The concept of pluralism implies seeing the very diversity of such a society, in terms for example of the range of religious experience and the variety of languages and language forms, as an enrichment of the experience of all those within it.   (p. 5)

In the late 1980s, in addition to the multicultural/multifaith approach exemplified by the Swann Report, a strand of thinking emerged, or re-emerged, which was to have a powerful effect on the imminent legislation. This strand might be termed the 'Christian heritage' lobby and it was essentially a combination of the Christian religious and the political 'right'. The former, largely those of evangelical or traditionalist views, saw acts of collective worship as a vehicle to promote Christian belief and were firmly confessional in approach. This was, in part, based on the belief that the Christian faith is true, and therefore it is right and proper to seek to nurture children into that faith. The political right (much of the Conservative party) saw acts of collective worship as a means of advocating a common moral and cultural basis for life based on the Christian heritage of the country. The debate between the 'multicultural' and 'Christian heritage' lobbies was to rage fiercely in the passage of the 1988 Education Reform Act.

The 1988 Education Reform Act

Out of this background emerged the 1988 Education Reform Act. This represented a political compromise between those who wished to follow the 'multicultural' path with its assumptions of mutual respect and tolerance for all views and its implicit relativism, and those who wished to stress the Christian heritage of Britain and maintain a strong position for the Christian faith in British schools. It is well known that the religious clauses were not part of the original legislation and were only included after the interventions of Baroness Cox and her supporters during the House of Lords' debates in an attempt to secure the predominance of Christianity in school R.E. and collective worship. The story of the passage of the bill through Parliament has been well documented (Alves 1991; Cox and Cairns 1989; Harte 1991; Hull 1989; Hull 1991; Robson 1996; Copley 1997; Chadwick 1997). The Bishop of London had acted as a broker during the passage of the bill in order to produce the end result. His comments on this process reflect the tensions between the 'Christian heritage' and 'multicultural' lobbies:

> Throughout the process of wrestling with the amendments we have tried to uphold five main principles. We have sought to provide a framework for worship which, first, maintains the tradition of worship as part of the process of education, giving proper place to the Christian religion; secondly, maintains the contribution of the collective act of worship to the establishment of values within the school community; yet, thirdly, does not impose inappropriate forms of worship on certain groups of pupils; fourthly, does not break the school up into communities based on the various faiths of the parents, especially in that it makes some groups feel that they are not really part of the community being educated in the school; and, lastly, is realisable and workable in practical terms of school accommodation and organisation.
>
> (*Hansard* 7.7.88 col. 434)

The main end results of the protracted and tortuous debates are as follows:

- the school's task included promoting the pupils' 'spiritual, moral, cultural, mental and physical development' and 'preparing them for the opportunities, responsibilities and experiences of adult life' [Education Reform Act 1988, section 1(2)]
- the daily act of collective worship was still required for all pupils, but it could now take place at any time in the school day and with any normal school group – e.g. a class, year or house [section 6(1) and (2)]
- worship was still not defined, but it must not be 'distinctive of any particular Christian denomination', and the majority of acts of collective worship must be 'wholly or mainly of a broadly Christian character' which meant that they should

reflect 'the broad traditions of Christian belief' [section 7(1), (2), (3)]

- schools could apply to the now mandatory local authority Standing Advisory Council on Religious Education (SACRE) for a 'determination' which released them from the last requirement (such a 'determination' would only last five years, after which it would have to be renewed) [sections 11 and 12]
- worship must have regard to the 'family background' and the 'ages and aptitudes' of the pupils involved [section 5]
- RE was outside the new 'National Curriculum' which prescribed certain standards in a range of compulsory subjects, but it maintained its special mandatory place by becoming part of what was now called the 'basic curriculum' which comprised the National Curriculum plus RE [section 2]
- the parental right to withdraw their child from collective worship and/or RE and the similar teachers' rights were unchanged from the 1944 Education Act.

The final wording of the Act was very much a political compromise between what might be termed the 'Christian heritage' and the 'multicultural' lobbies. The former can be seen in the continuing mandatory requirement for daily collective worship and for RE; in the inclusion of the word 'Christian' for the first time in law; and in the convoluted specification of the type of worship that was to be conducted in schools. The latter can be seen in the requirement that the character of the collective worship should take into account the 'family backgrounds', and 'ages and aptitudes' of the pupils; and in the provision for 'determinations'. In addition, the permission to hold the act of collective worship at any time in the school day and in school groups other than the entire school (although done, in part, for practical reasons) can be seen as a weakening of the role of collective worship in setting the tone and ethos for the whole school day.

The immediate aftermath to the 1988 Act

Whether or not the resulting legislation was a successful compromise which enacted the principles advocated by the Bishop of

London must be in severe doubt given the amount of controversy and confusion which followed the Act. The influential educational academic, Professor John Hull, argued that the Act was educationally and theologically unsound, and potentially divisive. He wrote that it was 'the most obscure and complicated piece of religious education legislation in the history of this country' (Hull 1989, p. 119). A study by Blight concluded that 'the 1988 worship requirements failed to address the key questions about the nature of modern society and the relationship between faith communities and schools and education and worship' (Blight 1994, p. 52). There was much concern in faith communities and schools as to how the Act was to be interpreted and a multitude of articles, booklets and guidelines appeared from educationalists, churches and other faith communities, teachers' unions and other professional associations, and local education authorities.

Important guidance came from Circular 3/89 in which the Department for Education and Science summarized the requirements of the 1988 Education Reform Act as regards RE and collective worship, and attempted to give some indication as to how the obscure phrase 'wholly or mainly of a broadly Christian character' was to be interpreted. It said, 'In the Secretary of State's view, an act of worship which is "broadly Christian" need not contain only Christian material provided that, taken as a whole, it reflects the traditions of Christian belief' (paragraph 34). It also suggested that 'governing bodies and headteachers should seek to respond positively' to requests from parents, whose children have been withdrawn from RE and/or collective worship, for the provision of religious education and/or religious worship 'according to a particular faith or denomination' provided there was no additional cost to the school (paragraph 42). This last piece of guidance can be seen as seeking to make allowance for the reality of a diversity of faiths.

The mountain of literature could not quell the unease. The Muslim community, in particular, was concerned about an emerging Christian imperialism. In a leaflet entitled *The Education Reform Act 1988: What Can Muslims do?* it was suggested that 'some of the changes regarding collective worship and religious education pose major challenges and immediate problems for Muslim parents' (Sarwar 1989, p. 1). Muslim parents were encouraged to send a letter of withdrawal from collective worship and RE to the headteacher of their child's school (p. 3). In addition, many evangelical Christian teachers were experiencing difficulty with multifaith RE and finding a real tension between their faith in Christ as the only saviour and their professional obligations to present other religions in an unbiased way (Association of Christian Teachers 1990). Both evangelical Christian and Muslim concerns since then have only grown stronger.

There was deep unease, too, among the teachers' unions and associations, especially the headteachers who had to shoulder much of the responsibility for the implementation of the Act. In July 1989 a *Times Educational Supplement* survey of headteachers produced only 1 out of 234 replies which expressed enthusiasm for the requirement that schools should hold a daily act of collective worship which is 'broadly or mainly Christian in character'. Furthermore 66 per cent said they had insufficient space for a whole school assembly and 61 per cent said they did not have the staff available to conduct Christian acts of worship. However, a major survey of heads of RE in all maintained secondary schools in England and Wales in the summer term of 1989 (with a 32 per cent response) showed a more varied and ambivalent attitude (Culham College Institute 1989). Despite considerable initial fears, there were not many legal cases brought against schools concerning the interpretation of the Act and such as there were proved largely inconclusive.

An emerging orthodoxy and orthopraxis in the early 1990s

Despite these serious concerns, most schools tried to work with the legislation and to make the most of it, and a critical examination of the literature and guidelines produced by the local authorities, faith groups, teachers and professional bodies suggests that a broad consensus was emerging on how to manage the vexed question of collective worship. This orthodoxy and orthopraxis suggested that collective worship has at least five main characteristics.

First, it is *sui generis* – a thing apart, of its own kind. McCreery wrote that collective worship 'is a form of worship which is peculiar to schools. It does not have its basis in any religious community, but the educational process of the school'

(McCreery 1993, p. 33). This is a continuation of the trend began with the 1870 Education Act with its requirement of non-denominational worship. Gent has commented that 'the reality is probably that schools are here being challenged to develop a unique kind of experience' (Gent 1989, p. 9).

Second, it is educational. Hughes and Collins commented that 'worship in the context of a school is first and foremost an educational activity' (1996, p. 8). For the most part it is assumed that the model of education is the liberal one. The aim is to broaden children's understanding and to make them more aware of and sensitive to different world-views to enable them to make their own informed choices at the appropriate time, based on reliable and comprehensive information and sound reasoning. The freedom and right of the individual to make their own personal choices in matters of religious belief is a basic axiom. This approach does not presume that any one religion is any more valid or true than any other. This all begs the questions of what is meant by 'education', what part the pursuit of truth plays in education, the issue of indoctrination and the place of nurturing religious belief in education, and the presumed epistemological status of religious truth claims. I shall return to these underlying issues in later chapters.

Third, collective worship is inclusive. As Gent puts it, 'It should be an activity and experience to which, in principle, *all* can contribute and from which *all* can gain, no matter what their personal commitment or life-stance' (Gent 1989, pp. 7–8). It is frequently emphasized that school worship is collective, not corporate – i.e. it is a gathering of people from many different cultural and religious backgrounds. This means that the response to an act of worship is left open; no particular belief or commitment is assumed. Often there will be a period of silence or 'thinking time' at the end rather than a traditional prayer with all its implicit assumptions. The BBC *Together* programme (a radio assembly for schools) very deliberately takes into account the variety of cultural, social and religious backgrounds and the different levels of belief commitment, and so aims to allow response 'on several levels'. The Secondary Heads Association has published a book of assembly ideas called *Thought for the Day* in which the 'thought' is simply followed by a corporate silence to allow for a variety of responses (Douglas 1995). The inclusivity requirement also means that material from many different sources is used including various faith traditions and other world-views. Many schools make use of the multifaith *Shap Calendar of Religious Festivals* when planning their assembly programme. School worship involves 'celebrating' the diversity of world-views, particularly those represented in the school. In addition, attitudes of tolerance, sensitivity, respect, understanding and awareness are encouraged towards the variety of beliefs. The National Union of Teachers' guidance given in 1989 said:

> The Union, whilst supporting the right of parents to withdraw their children on religious grounds, does not want to see a divisive spirit of intolerance grow up amongst different faiths in the school community – schools should be helping to foster tolerance and respect throughout their educational work, and in the past assemblies have played an important part in this.   (National Union of Teachers 1989, p. 8)

The emphasis on developing these attitudes in the interests of inclusivity can be so strong that the questions of different, contradictory or even unacceptable beliefs are sidelined, as is the issue of the truth of religious beliefs.

Fourth, the powerful desire to have an occasion which includes the whole school community in all its diversity of beliefs and cultures means that there is frequently an emphasis on perceived common or shared values and school ethos and tone. This is very much in line with the Department for Education Circular 1/94 which states that collective worship should 'develop community spirit, promote a common ethos and shared values, and reinforce positive attitudes' (paragraph 50). The same circular also requires schools to encourage children to develop 'a clear set of personal values and beliefs' (paragraph 9). This raises the question of the relative status of the common and personal values. How do they interact? Who decides what the common values will be? There is a fundamental paradox here: schools are being asked to provide pupils with the means to construct their own values and beliefs (and not to presume the truth or validity of any particular view), whilst simultaneously promoting a school ethos which is based on perceived common values. Are the common values restricted to desired modes of behaviour, or do they include common beliefs about the nature and purpose of human life? If so, then where does the question of the truth and validity of these common values and beliefs fit into this system which is so anxious to avoid making judgements about the beliefs of individuals?

Fifth, the current orthodoxy and orthopraxis are based on a 'worth-ship' model of collective worship. The definition of worship is seen, not in the narrow religious sense of offering worship to a transcendent God, but in the broader sense of valuing things considered to be of ultimate worth or value. This often means giving opportunity for developing a sense of awe and wonder, reflection on various human values and ideals, celebration of achievements of various kinds, and for exploring our inner 'spirituality'. Frequently, this broad definition of worship leads to the focus of the worship being immanent rather than transcendent (i.e. the focus is on this world and its directly observable aspects), and this typically takes the form of a moral emphasis rather than a religious one. Copley speaks of 'the rise of the secular sermon' to describe the trend towards moral homilies which has been particularly prevalent in secondary schools (Copley 1989a, p. 28). Part of the reason for this is that there seems to be far greater agreement on certain moral values than there is on religious beliefs.

The current orthodoxy and orthopraxis is widely and well documented. It is well summed up in Copley's 'thought for the day' model (Copley 1989a, pp. 32–43) where he says that school worship should:

- accept all beliefs as valid
- encourage tolerance and respect
- recognize pluralism
- entail the leader expressing a viewpoint and offering it for reflection
- not presume any particular response or belief in the participants.

Reactions to the orthodoxy and orthopraxis

As time went by in the 1990s it became increasingly clear that this fragile consensus did not appeal to everyone. The trend in recent years has been toward greater polarization in views rather than consensus. Crudely speaking, both sides of the debate have sought to strengthen their position in different ways.

There had been dissatisfaction from the 'Christian heritage' lobby that the Act had not done enough to reinforce the nation's traditional Christian foundation as expressed in school worship. There were two very significant developments with regard to the way in which the law was to be implemented and interpreted which swung the balance distinctly in the direction of the 'Christian heritage' lobby. The first was the issuing of Circular 1/94 by the DFE which sought to give guidance and interpretation concerning RE and collective worship. It said that although school worship was not defined in the legislation it 'should be concerned with reverence or veneration paid to a divine being or power' (paragraph 57), and should 'aim to provide an opportunity for pupils to worship God' (paragraph 50). It must also 'contain some elements which relate specifically to the traditions of Christian belief and which accord a special status to Jesus Christ' (paragraph 63). The second development was the *Ofsted Inspection Schedule* issued in 1995 which aimed to help inspectors form their judgements about the 'character and quality of worship in schools'. They were told that 'worship is generally understood to imply a recognition of a supreme being'. In addition, 'it should be clear that the words used and/or the activities observed in worship recognise the existence of a deity', and that 'if the worship consistently avoids reference to Jesus within the spoken or written word then it could not reasonably be defined as mainly Christian . . .' Both of these attempts to insist on the Christian character of school worship have been widely resented and opposed, particularly by the teaching organizations.

There was a storm of outrage amongst the multicultural lobby that an ideology of Christian imperialism was at work. In the 1993 Hockerill Lecture John Hull argued that the draft of what was to become Circular 1/94 reflected a 'government departmental theology' which had emerged in the previous five years. This theology was characterized by:

- the desire to teach religions as discrete units, which led to the marginalization of religions other than Christianity
- an emphasis on Christianity as integral to British national heritage, which was divisive and took little account of the contemporary multicultural realities
- the view that Christianity must predominate.

Hull argued that this government 'theology' was educationally flawed and morally offensive (Hull 1993).

Another important twist in the story comes from the growing critiques of liberal education coming from at least four directions: evangelical Christians, the Muslim community, postmodern perspectives, and from philosophical viewpoints. These critiques will be explored in more depth in later chapters, but we should note at this point that they suggest that the questions of the nature of religious belief, the competing truth claims of the different religions and world-views, and how this should be handled in an educational context all need to be explored in relation to collective worship in schools if a satisfactory policy is ever to be developed out of the present quagmire.

There have been some serious efforts to find an acceptable way forward for collective worship. The most recent and comprehensive attempt at consultation took place in 1997 and produced three possible ways forward (R.E. Council et al. 1998, pp. 22, 36):

- a 'new way forward' based on a statutory requirement for regular assemblies of a moral and spiritual character, with the present requirement for collective worship being withdrawn
- maintenance of the present requirements either entirely or substantially in their present form
- the withdrawal of the present requirements without replacement.

Most of the teachers' bodies and local authority groups favoured the first option, but there were considerable reservations amongst the faith communities. The divisions and disagreements remained and still remain as profound as ever.

Conclusion

Since 1997 there have been some important developments in the legal framework for collective worship. However, most of this maintains the basic thrust and principles expounded in the 1988 Education Reform Act, but applies them to the increasing diversity of types of publicly funded school. The 1998 School Standards and Framework Act introduced the ideas of foundation and community schools in addition to voluntary aided and voluntary controlled schools. The Education Act 2002 developed the concept of academies as publicly funded independent schools sponsored by business, faith or voluntary groups.

There have also been some notable changes in the approach of Ofsted in the guidance given for school inspections. In Ofsted *Update 42* (August 2003) inspectors were told that a failure to provide a daily act of collective worship was a significant breach of statute and, since one of the duties of a governing body is to ensure that a school meets its statutory obligations, this short-coming meant that the governance of a school should be judged unsatisfactory. In response to complaints from schools, revised guidance was issued in *Update 43*. This reduced the requirement for satisfactory governance to showing that the governing body had 'done all it reasonably could to ensure compliance'. In the light of continuing non-compliance, and the changing religious make-up of the UK, the Chief Inspector of Schools, David Bell, has, in April 2004, become the latest in a long line of those calling for a change in legislation. In this case he argued for a less frequent requirement for worship (weekly or even monthly rather than daily), and for a revision of the guidance in Circular 1/94, which says that broadly Christian worship should be taken as meaning including veneration for a divine being or power, and also some elements that accord a special status to Jesus Christ.

The liberal consensus and the framework of modernity have had a profound hold on the system of education. However, the advent of a plural and postmodern society means that this consensus is breaking down. In addition the Christian heritage of the UK has a much less overt influence over public life than was once the case. This has generated deep questions concerned with finding appropriate ways of understanding and treating different religious beliefs and world-views in the complex situation of the twenty-first century. These questions are focused very sharply in the particular situation of collective worship in schools. The current framework for collective worship is a result of a multi-tude of compromises over many years. The result of this is that the teachers involved in leading collective worship are in a frontier situation trying to work out how competing beliefs and ideologies can live together. A careful examination of the profound sociological, ethical, theological and educational issues which underlie collective worship is essential both for schools and for wider society.

CHAPTER 3

Sociological Issues

Introduction

Teachers in many a primary school in the 1950s would have been very grateful for publications such as the *Junior Teacher's Assembly Book*. It provided an invaluable supply of prayers, readings and themes (Prescott 1953). The typical assembly at the start of the school day involved an opening sentence, a prayer, a reading (almost always from the Bible), a reflection on the theme, a hymn and a closing sentence. The vast majority of this material was drawn from the Christian faith with very little, if anything, from other faiths or world-views. The clear assumption was that the majority of the children could be considered as at least nominal Christians and many would have some attachment to a church. There was no doubt that the Christian faith provided the basic framework for assemblies and there was very little provision for the small number of pupils of other faiths.

At the beginning of the twenty-first century the situation is very different. Teachers are acutely aware of the variety of beliefs and world-views represented in a school assembly. The style of assemblies is no longer that of a watered-down church service, but is much more diverse both in form and content. Teachers now draw from a multitude of sources, religious and non-religious, to construct a whole variety of assembly formats which recognize the range of beliefs which may be present – see, for example, the material on the website <www.assemblies.org.uk>.

No account of collective worship can ignore the massive changes which have taken place in British culture and society, particularly since the Second World War. The 1944 Education Act more or less assumed that it was the task of schools to nurture children in the Christian faith to enable them to take part in the worshipping life of the churches. By 1970, with the impact of declining church attendance and the process of secularization, the Church of England's Durham Report (*The Fourth R*), which explored the place of religious education in schools, described England as a 'post ecclesiastical society', implying that most people were no longer linked formally to the institutional Church in any meaningful way. By 1985 the influence of immigration was well established. This brought not only a greater diversity of people into the Christian churches, but also those of other faiths were present in far larger numbers in many areas of the UK. The 1985 government-sponsored Swann Report (*Education for All*) was emphatic in encouraging a positive attitude to plurality and diversity and in promoting greater understanding and mutual respect between cultures. The recognition that Britain was a country with a multiplicity of beliefs and non-beliefs was now centre-stage: multicultural Britain had come of age. The effect of this on the once dominant place of Christianity is ambiguous. By 2000 one academic, Callum Brown, was talking of 'the death of Christian Britain' (Brown 2001), and yet in the 2001 national census 72 per cent of the population were still describing their religion as Christian, and another survey in that year found that over one third of the population had attended a Christmas church service. These and other changes in attitudes to the place of religious belief in contemporary society have been massive, but also extremely complex. In many important respects these changes are reflected in the ways in which school assembly patterns have altered over the years, and to have a clear account of them is crucial for the way we understand what is going on in collective worship today.

Insights from sociological studies and surveys

Several recent sociological studies (e.g. the national census of 2001; the European Values Survey 1999/2000; Davie 1994; Bruce 1995; Woodhead and Heelas 2000) have sought to describe and analyse what is happening to religious belief in contemporary Britain. We do need to recognize that there is a vast amount we simply do not know about the nature of people's deep beliefs, religious or otherwise; Woodhead and Heelas (2000, p. 1) warn that 'religion in modern times remains relatively uncharted territory'. However, there are at least four key themes which we can draw from these sociological studies:

- the phenomenon of believing in some faith, or a variant of it, without belonging to a religious institution
- the way in which religious belief is treated as a matter for private, individual choice and the impact of this on the understanding of that belief
- the differences between various age groups in attitudes to religion
- the impact of the events of September 11, 2001.

The first of these themes is what the sociologist of religion Grace Davie (1994, p. 5) calls 'persistent undercurrents of faith'. She summarizes the findings of several surveys in the telling phrase 'believing without belonging'. There is a growing mismatch between the evidence for various kinds of religious belief in this country, which remains relatively strong, and the statistics which show a marked decline in religious membership and practice – at least as regards the institutional churches. The sacred persists, but not necessarily in traditional forms. Religious belief is mutating rather than disappearing. As Davie says, it is more accurate 'to describe late-twentieth century Britain – together with the rest of Europe – as unchurched rather than simply secular' (pp. 12–13). In the second half of the twentieth century, surveys suggest that a generalized belief in God remained fairly constant at around 70 per cent of the population. This trend has continued into the twenty-first century as witnessed by the 2001 national census which gives only 16 per cent of the population as stating they have 'no religion'. The latest (1999/2000) European Values Study (see Halman et al. 2001) has indicated that while church attendance in Europe continues to decline (from 30 per cent once a month in 1990 to 25 per cent in 2000), belief in a personal God is rising in some countries and only 5 per cent say they are atheists.

The second important feature for us to note from the sociological studies is the way in which religious belief in the late twentieth and early twenty-first centuries has become seen as primarily a matter of private, individual choice. This has a major impact on how that belief is formulated and expressed. The most helpful metaphor to illustrate this is that of religious consumerism.

We shop around for our spiritual needs and nowadays a variety of products are available. Some are from the traditional churches and other major world religions, whilst some are newer products such as the so-called 'New Age' beliefs and practices. Yet others can be produced by an individual 'pick 'n' mix' approach – choosing particular elements from different faiths and combining them in a way which suits the individual concerned. Grace Davie has described this phenomenon as a change in the approach to religion from seeing it as a matter of common obligation to a matter of personal consumption. Religious beliefs and views are now no longer part of the public, 'taken-for-granted' world; rather they are largely the preserve of committed minorities who are members of a multitude of private interest clubs. One of the crucial effects of this is a relativizing of attitudes towards religions – i.e. a tendency to say that in this realm it is perfectly acceptable for each person to make his or her own choices and that one choice is as valid as any other. These comments are endorsed by the findings of the European Values Study (1981–1990, and 1999/2000). Secularization is still a strong trend with the place of institutional religion declining in people's lives. Confidence in all institutions, including the churches, is also waning. Individualism – the freedom to choose in every area of life – is highly valued, as is autonomy – the freedom of people to 'act according to their own (divergent) norms' (European Values Group 1992, p. 6). As far as religious and other world-views are concerned the picture is one of fragmentation, individualization and relativism. This trend has continued in the 1999/2000 survey results. This major transition has been likened to the loss of a common language, and the Chief Rabbi, Jonathan Sacks (1995, p. vii), has commented that 'with the transition of Britain from a strong common culture to a more fragmented, segmented and pluralized one, we suddenly find we are all members of a minority group'.

The third major feature which we must note from the sociological studies is the influence of age on attitudes to religious belief. The European Values Survey (1992) found that 'values are generationally and perhaps also age related, at least to some extent . . . 64% of the people who are over 50 years of age consider religion to be important in their lives, whereas for people under the age of 35, only 34% consider it to be important' (p. 52). Very significantly, 'only one in seven parents aged under

35 years believes that it is important to develop religious faith in children' (p. 9). Their findings suggest that 'younger generations are significantly less likely than older generations to have had a religious upbringing or to regard religion as important in life' (p. 44). In a questionnaire survey of over thirteen thousand young people aged between thirteen and fifteen Francis and Kay (1995, p. 136) found that 'nearly two out of five (39%) are theists and a similar number (35%) are agnostics. Atheists amount to a quarter (26%)'. They also reported that, 'the view that Christianity is the only true religion is held by only 16% of teenagers and rejected by 42%. The remaining 42% are uncertain about this' (p. 137). The figures for Sunday School attendance are also highly significant. In the 1930s approximately two-thirds of all children attended; by the 1950s this was down to about one half. By the early 1990s only about 15 per cent of children had any kind of a link to the institutional Church (General Synod Board of Education and Board of Mission 1991, p. 4). The key question is whether or not these changes represent a permanent shift in behaviour and attitude which will persist into adulthood and old age. Davie (2000, p. 180) notes that 'the younger generations of Europe have effectively lost touch with the institutional churches . . . and . . . the forms of religious instruction provided in the educational systems of modern Europe are moving away from a model based on catechesis to modes of teaching that offer information about rather than in religious beliefs'. The result of this is what she describes as the 'precariousness' of the memory of Christian belief and tradition in Europe. In other words, will the residual Christian heritage of Britain survive another generation?

A fourth substantial factor in attitudes towards religious belief in contemporary Britain has been the massive impact of the events of September 11, 2001. There is constant debate and analysis, but for our purposes there are at least two main features of which to take note. The first is that religious belief, particularly in its more fundamentalist form, is now firmly back in the public eye and in the public arena. The idea that it could be consigned totally to the domain of the private and individual has been shown to be wanting. From a Muslim point of view the distinction between the private life of the individual and the public corporate sphere has never been valid. Many Christians and people from other faiths would also want to challenge that distinction. Their faith is about all of life, not just a personal inner attitude or private hobby with no implications for public life. The second impact of the events of September 11, 2001 is a much increased fear of the potential of religion as a cause of division and strife. The talk of a 'clash of civilizations', the thesis put forward by Samuel Huntington, has fuelled concerns of a radical split between Muslim understandings and those of the so-called 'western world'. Another manifestation of the same theme can be found in the widespread fears that faith schools, which have been actively promoted in recent years both by the faith communities and by government policy, are deeply divisive. The longer-term influence of these features is as yet unknown, but there is little doubt that it is significant.

These findings from sociological studies suggest that very substantial changes are taking place in the understanding of religious beliefs and the part such beliefs play in people's lives. Although we need to be cautious about broad-brush descriptions of previous eras, there has been a shift from a more homogeneous society in which Christianity played a more central role to a more heterogeneous one in which Christianity exists alongside other major faiths and world-views as well as 'New Age' beliefs. This coexists with an awareness of the power of religion for both good and ill, and that it cannot be quietly consigned to the private domain.

The shift from modernity to postmodernity

Another important contour of contemporary society which is highly relevant to the sociological context of collective worship is the much debated shift from modernity to postmodernity. Modernity is an extremely complex social, economic, political and philosophical phenomenon which had its origins in the Enlightenment and has dominated western culture ever since, although there are significant indications that we are now at a moment of major cultural transition to what has been called 'postmodernity'. We need to note some of the key themes of modernity because they have substantially shaped our present understandings of truth, knowledge, religious belief and education – all of which are central to our subject. Indeed, Usher and Edwards (1994, p. 2) have gone so far as to suggest that

Educational theory and practice is founded on the discourse of modernity [. . .]. Historically, education can be seen as the vehicle by which modernity's 'grand narratives', the Enlightenment ideals of critical reason, individual freedom, progress and benevolent change, are substantiated and realised.

The crucial themes of modernity which are relevant for us include:

- the emphasis on the individual as the knowing subject as expressed by the seventeenth-century philosopher Descartes (the so-called 'father of modern philosophy')
- the empiricism which sought knowledge via the senses and human experience rather than via divine revelation
- the confidence in an overarching, universal reason which was context- and culture-neutral
- the enormous influence of science which became the effective paradigm of true, objective knowledge built on empirical 'facts' and the use of inductive and analytic reason
- the assigning of religious belief to the 'private' domain and the rights and freedom of the individual to make their own choices in such matters.

There have been several important critiques of what has been termed 'the Enlightenment Project'. The scientist Michael Polanyi (1958) questioned the concept of detached, objective knowledge, arguing that individual and personal perspectives can never be eliminated from what we claim to know. Moral philosopher Alasdair MacIntyre (especially 1985a and 1988) emphasized the socially embodied character of traditions of rationality – i.e. the communities which we inhabit affect the way we think and our rules of discourse and reason.

Many scholars and other commentators argue that the western world is in the midst of a major shift from modernity to postmodernity (e.g. Connor 1989; Middleton and Walsh 1995; Osborn 1995; Anderson ed. 1996). This transition has affected virtually all areas of life and it includes both sociological and philosophical aspects. There are several important themes of which we must take note. These include the following:

- a suspicion of 'metanarratives', i.e. grand overarching explanatory systems of thought or belief

- the nature of world-views as constructs of the human mind, with the consequence that there are many such world-views, all equally valid
- the relativization of truth, often seeing claims to the 'Truth' as a covert exercise of unwarranted power
- an emphasis on the plurality of voices and views, and the existence of 'multiple language games' or 'systems of meaning'
- the idea that we live in a 'centreless universe' with no safely detached observation posts from which human life and thought can be evaluated in any absolute manner
- that we have moved away from the Enlightenment confidence in human 'Reason' towards a realization that there are many different types of rationality, not necessarily all commensurable
- that each individual is free to choose and construct their own world-view and version of reality.

This transition from modernity to postmodernity can be seen in some of the changes to the school curriculum. A pupil of the 1950s would have been taught a much more uniform approach to, say, history or English literature than a pupil of the twenty-first century. The latter would be made very aware of the multitude of interpretations and vantage points from which the world can be seen – e.g. feminist, black, the poor, etc. There is no completely objective, detached point of view.

The reflection of these trends in contemporary collective worship

Not surprisingly the practice of collective worship has been significantly affected by these seismic shifts in attitudes to religious belief. In particular, in my research there were two extremely important themes. The first was a substantial emphasis by the teachers who led collective worship on individual freedom of choice in matters of religious and other world-views. The second theme was the counter-balancing of this stress on the individual by a strong desire to find places of unity and common ground in the midst of the diversity of our plural culture – usually this unity was sought in the area of so-called 'common values', or in an understanding of our common humanity.

Individual freedom of choice

We are very familiar with the idea of consumer choice. This is a concept which is written deeply into the fabric of the modern western world. It can be extended far beyond the choices we make in the supermarket. Nowadays we expect to be able to choose our beliefs and lifestyles from the bewildering variety which abounds in our plural world, and if there is none that suits our needs we can then 'pick 'n' mix' to construct a pattern that will work for us. This emphasis on freedom of choice for each individual was illustrated in at least two different ways in my research data: first, in allowing an 'open' response to whatever thoughts or ideas were expressed in collective worship; and second, in emphasizing individual choice in matters of world-views and stressing the right to believe different things.

Most teachers were well aware of the paradoxical nature of collective worship. On the one hand the word 'collective' implies that people are collected together and makes no assumptions about the beliefs or attitudes of those people: on the other hand the word 'worship' is usually taken to imply a certain type of belief and commitment. This paradox has been commented upon and analysed at great length (e.g. Hull 1975, chapters 2 and 3; Roger 1982, p. 154). In order to handle this paradoxical situation all the teachers interviewed took considerable care to allow an 'open' response to what was being said or done in collective worship. This meant that they made no assumptions, at least in terms of religious belief, on behalf of those present; nor did they seek to elicit any particular response of worship, but tried to ensure that individuals could make their own free response in their own terms. One infant school headteacher expressed this by stressing the importance of giving the children 'space to be what they want to be'. Such an emphasis on openness of response occurred in the vast majority of the schools, and for most acts of collective worship the material was presented in such a way as to allow a variety of possible responses, of which worship could be one for those who wished it. One infant headteacher said, 'the worship part is a time when I hope every child, if they want to worship and if they understand, [knows] that they can worship in their own way . . . I want them to be able to worship in their own religion'. The implication seems to be that each child will make an individual and internal response, which may or may not be one of worship, to what is presented by the leader of the act of collective worship. This raises major questions about the extent to which children are equipped to make such a response, especially given that relatively little empirical work has been done on the spiritual life of children (Hay and Nye 1998, esp. p.v).

All the school policies in my sample emphasized the centrality of an open individual response to the act of collective worship – i.e. one not prescribed by the leader (although in the Catholic school this was often seen in terms of faith development). No school wished to compromise anyone's sincerely held beliefs or force them into an activity about which they had reservations or objections. All of them wished to allow pupils a genuinely open choice in matters of belief. The need to allow an open response in collective worship and not to presume anything on the part of either pupils or teachers in terms of personal beliefs and attitudes also appears in the government and local authority documents. Circular 1/94 (DFE 1994, paragraph 59) says, 'an act of collective worship should be capable of eliciting a response from pupils, even though on a particular occasion some of the pupils may not feel able actively to identify with the act of worship'. This approach of allowing an open response is in keeping with many of the guidelines issued concerning collective worship. For example, the national Churches' Joint Educational Policy Committee (CJEPC) statement said

> the school is no place for either indoctrination or woolly openness. If worship is to be a free activity . . . its observance must allow both its leader and the pupils to respect each other's integrity and freedom. This requires an open atmosphere which creates the opportunity for, but does not dictate, a particular response.
>
> (CJEPC 1995, paragraph 2.5.3)

In a similar vein, Brown and Furlong (1996, p. 18) say that if worship is to contribute to the spiritual development of pupils it should be

> always inviting, never coercing, remembering that pupils will be at different stages of spiritual development and that

they should feel able to respond and participate at their own level.

Most teachers also stressed the importance of the children making up their minds at some stage on their own beliefs and values. This is well illustrated by the following quotations from my interviews: 'it's . . . a matter for the children whether they believe it or not. I try to give them an open-ended aspect of it' (a primary teacher); 'I don't think I am responsible for the choices they make' (secondary school teacher); 'at the end of the day it's their choice whether they choose to believe or not' (junior school teacher). All the teachers interviewed acknowledged the importance of this free choice of the individual pupil. They did this in various different ways – for example in the way prayer or reflection was introduced, by the use of story, through encouragement to reflect upon personal values and beliefs, by a stress on education as enhancing choice, and by avoiding perceived indoctrination.

The government and local authority documents also emphasize the individual's freedom of choice. The 1988 Education Reform Act and Circular 3/89 deal with this by providing the possibility of withdrawal from collective worship by individual pupils or teachers, and 'determinations' by schools to lift the requirement that the worship shall be 'wholly or mainly of a broadly Christian character'; and also by stressing that the character of collective worship shall take into account 'the family backgrounds of the pupils concerned' and 'their ages and aptitudes' (1988 ERA sections 7, 12). This official encouragement of pupils to develop their own personal beliefs and values in a freely chosen way is reinforced by the Ofsted inspection criteria which require inspectors to make judgements which 'are concerned with the opportunities given for pupils to learn about and explore different values, beliefs and views and to develop and express their own' (Ofsted 1995c, p. 89).

It is important to note that this freedom of choice to develop personal values, beliefs and views was not all it seemed to be. It mostly applied in the area of religious beliefs; when it came to moral beliefs such openness was not there in the same way. It seemed to be axiomatic that it was not part of the school's task to encourage children into any particular faith, but with regard to morality and matters of pupil behaviour there was a much more absolutist stance as I shall explore in more depth in the following chapters. This open attitude to religious belief is illustrated by the following quotation from a Church of England junior school teacher: 'To say "you must believe this" in a school is not acceptable. I would say to a child "my choice is to believe this, you may choose to believe this," but to say "you must believe this" would be wholly unacceptable.' The strength of feeling behind this statement was very strong – individual freedom of choice in religious belief was an educational canon in this case. A Muslim teacher expressed the importance of freedom of choice as follows:

> My idea of living in Britain is that we have people of different faiths and everybody is free to choose whatever path they want to walk on. And the rest of us we should respect and value them for that.
>
> I tell people that Muslims believe in one God, that there's only one sort of creation, and I tell people that we believe in accountability, and that we believe in the prophets; and if people can find sense in that then it's up to them whether or not to accept Islam.

The importance of freedom of belief and the right of individual pupils to make their own choices was summed up succinctly by an infant school teacher who said, 'we live where people can believe different things and it comes back to choices again'. This freedom to believe different things is enshrined in article 18 of the 1948 United Nations Universal Declaration of Human Rights which says:

> Everyone has the right to freedom of thought, conscience and religion; this right includes the right to change his religion or belief, and freedom either alone or in community with others and in public or private, to manifest his religion or belief in teaching, practice, worship and observance.

The teachers' approach is superficially in accord with this declaration although, as we shall see later, the position is complicated by three main factors: first, the implicit desire of some to nurture; second, the dominant place of Christianity in collective worship; and, third, ironically, the dominant position of liberal education which can suppress the free expression of viewpoints other than that of liberalism.

Four illustrations of the desire for individual freedom of choice

The importance of allowing an open response and free choice was particularly well illustrated in four ways in the actual practice of collective worship:

- the use of prayer or reflection
- the use made of stories
- the emphasis on personal development
- the strong desire of teachers that material used in assemblies should be relevant and useful to the pupils.

Each of these will now be considered.

The use of prayer or reflection

The desire to allow an open response is vividly shown in the approach taken to prayer or reflection by most teachers. This was an important aspect of collective worship and was used in one form or another by all those interviewed, although with varying degrees of enthusiasm and in diverse forms. In the interviews many said that they did not often use the prescriptive formula, 'Let us pray', on the grounds that it presumes too much about the likely response of those present, who may or may not believe in a god, and who may or may not want to pray at that moment in time. They preferred a less prescriptive introduction or a simple invitation to reflect upon what has been said. The following quotations (both from junior school teachers) from my interviews illustrate this approach: 'I usually miss out what I myself would call prayer. I tend to say, "Would you like to think about it?" because I don't like to say to children, "We are now going to pray". . . you have to be very careful how you word it to them'; 'I just say "This is a prayer", . . . or I might say "I would like you to close your eyes and just think about these words that I am going to say"'. This approach is in line with that advocated by the Churches' Joint Educational Policy Committee statement on collective worship which said:

> As with prayers, however, so with hymns or songs – pupils (and staff) should be allowed to observe or to be silent and not be expected to say or sing anything which would be insincerely uttered.

Equally the willing pupil should be allowed – even encouraged – to make a sincere contribution.

(CJEPC 1995, Annex 'A', point (e))

In some teachers a tension was evident between the need to have openness of response and the desire to have some Christian prayers. One infant teacher acknowledged the diversity of faiths in her school and the need for them not to be compromised. She said: 'I think if they are going to be comfortable they have got to be able to pray in their own way . . . I do try in the general run of assemblies to have a prayer that mentions God. We have one other prayer that begins, "Father, we thank you for the night, and for the pleasant morning light", and sometimes I feel a little bit uneasy about that one.' The unease in this case stemmed from the fact that the word 'Father' was a specifically Christian title for God, and she did not want to 'threaten the other children'. And yet this had to be held in tension with the fact that 'the prayers have to be Christian. It's important that they are Christian . . . because a lot of the children are Christian, it's a school in England and the assemblies are meant to be mostly Christian.'

This tension was further illustrated in the actual practice of leading prayer in collective worship. The observations told a rather different story to the professed allegiance to openness which I have just illustrated from the main interviews. In 18 out of 35 infant and junior acts of collective worship the teacher said a prayer addressed to God with little introduction other than the formula, 'Let us pray'. In only nine of these assemblies was the introduction of the more open type which the teachers described in the interviews. It seemed that there was an approved 'open' method in the intentions of the teachers and in the school policies, but in practice the teachers' habits or beliefs proved stronger. It is likely that although most teachers acknowledged the importance of recognizing the diversity of beliefs and the need for openness, nevertheless deeply ingrained habits sometimes shaped by their own beliefs still moulded what they actually did in collective worship. This led some teachers in a direction which was more confessional than open and liberal.

There was a distinct difference between the primary and the secondary schools in the approach to prayer. In the former prayer seemed to be far more frequent and much more likely to be couched in the terminology of a conventional prayer. In the latter the tendency was to use silent reflection far more: if a prayer was used the teacher normally gave a careful introduction. This approach is well illustrated in the following comments from secondary school teachers: 'We had one Head of Year who on occasions has said, "I am now going to read a prayer, for some of you this will be a way of expressing your Christian thought, for others of you the words can be used how you want to"'; 'I've never used the word "prayer". I might use it and say this is a prayer written by somebody who was a Christian and felt they were able to say this, but I wouldn't actually use it for them to pray'; 'Silence, yes, prayers very rarely'. The county secondary school collective worship policies in my research sample all stressed the use of times of quiet personal reflection rather than prayer – e.g. 'Time will be provided each day for pupils to spend in quiet reflection . . . Assembly leaders end assembly with a general thought or prayer or they ask pupils to reflect upon the assembly theme.' Another policy spoke of 'creating an atmosphere of quiet reflection'. Yet another said that assembly aimed at 'providing a break from the busy-ness of life (the "pause before the plunge")'.

The use of stories

Another illustration of the desire to emphasize freedom of individual choice is found in the importance of stories in assembly for many teachers. This was not only because the children would follow them, but also because stories allowed a response at many different levels. One junior school teacher said she coped with the diversity of beliefs 'basically by being the story-teller' because story was open-ended. Another such teacher described the 'open' character of stories by saying, 'there are all sorts of slants you can take from one story and pick up umpteen strands from it.' The importance and openness of stories were expressed by yet another junior school teacher who said: 'I try to tell them a story that they will enjoy. There's always a story element with mine.' A crucial part of story for this teacher was 'not being preached at'. The use of story was much more pronounced in the infant and junior schools where 12 out of 24 teachers stressed it; in the secondary schools only one teacher out of 13 mentioned it. Part of the reason for this marked difference would be pedagogical – more styles of presentation would be open to the secondary school teacher dealing with older children.

Personal development of beliefs

Freedom of choice was further illustrated in all the data by a strong theme which emphasized the development of personal beliefs and values. This was usually seen in highly individualistic terms, thereby reflecting the findings of the sociological surveys which suggested that religious belief is largely regarded as an individual and private affair. There were many comments from teachers which illustrated this. One Catholic secondary school teacher sought to 'guide them and help them formulate their own opinions . . . and how they are going to live their life'. He said later: 'That's one of the aims of assemblies – to try and get the depth of reflection and thought increasing.' Reflection was a key theme for one junior school teacher who said, 'I keep going back to this reflective bit. I think it is terribly important to give them an opportunity to think about things.' The theme of reflection and thinking about basic values was particularly strong in the secondary schools. This was illustrated by the comment of one teacher who said of assembly: 'It's almost a place where you can hold something . . . up for examination and just even to pose the question and say, here is this, what do you think about it. Not give them any answers necessarily, but, here is this idea, think about it.'

All the secondary school collective worship policies contained this theme of individual and personal development. It embraced a sense of self-worth and identity, and personal values and development. The infant and junior policy documents also all wanted to contribute to the personal development of the children – spiritual, moral, social and cultural. Frequently the concept of spiritual development was seen as something which transcended all beliefs. One junior school's policy stated: 'Spiritual development . . . transcends the potential barriers of religious and cultural difference . . . spiritual growth is not dependent on a child having a secure faith background.' The spiritual was seen as concerned with a person's 'inner life' and with 'basic human questions'. Government and local authority guidelines also contained a strong emphasis on the development of the individual. The 1988

Education Reform Act [section 1.(2)] stipulated that the curriculum of the school should be one which

(a) promotes the spiritual, moral, cultural, mental and physical development of pupils at the school and of society; and
(b) prepares such pupils for the opportunities, responsibilities and experiences of adult life.

Spiritual development is not defined in this Act, but is explored in other government documents, notably from Ofsted and the then School Curriculum and Assessment Authority (SCAA). Here it was usually seen in terms of individuals forging their own views and beliefs in a freely chosen way. The school's task in this process was not to impose or dictate, but to provide information and understanding so that pupils were enabled to make informed choices. For example, Ofsted inspectors are to look for evidence of 'whether pupils are encouraged to articulate their own views and beliefs' (Ofsted 1995b, p. 62), and whether the school 'seeks to enrich its pupils' knowledge and experience of their own and other cultural traditions' (Ofsted 1995b, p. 85).

The importance of using relevant and meaningful material

The final illustration from the data of the emphasis on individual freedom of choice was provided by the strong desire of the teachers for collective worship to be an occasion which was meaningful and relevant to the children – as one teacher put it 'something to connect to'. Twenty-three out of 24 infant and junior school teachers and eight out of 13 secondary school teachers stressed the importance of relevance and accessibility in the assembly material. The following comments from the interviews illustrate this concern and were typical of many: 'you can talk to them about things that relate to them . . . I've tried to bring things to their level' (junior school teacher); 'something that connects' (secondary school teacher); 'linking it to what's going on in their daily lives . . . grounded in something that's . . . a concrete issue with them' (church secondary school teacher). In all the assemblies observed it was clear that the teachers gave a high priority to providing material and stimulus which related directly to the children's world.

All teachers wanted to achieve relevance and to use accessible material. A survey of secondary school pupils in East Yorkshire by Bryan (1997) suggested that most pupils found assembly irrelevant and uninteresting. At its lowest level this desire by teachers for relevance can be seen as a survival tactic. A few hundred bored children cooped together in a hall with only a handful of teachers is not a happy prospect for the leader of collective worship! This desire may also stem from an emphasis on experiential learning reflecting the work of Loukes on RE in the 1960s. Loukes (1961) argued that RE should begin with issues and problems which were of concern to the pupils and only then build links to Christian and biblical teaching. He called this the 'problem method'. Many of the older teachers would have been trained at a time when the ideas of Loukes were very influential in RE. Hull (1984) has argued in a related way that a theological rationale for collective worship should begin with the child's concerns and only then proceed to matters of 'ultimate concern' (drawing on the theology of Tillich). Hull said:

> School worship does not bite sufficiently deeply into the genuine concerns of pupils . . . Our task in school assembly then is to take the most transparent, the most symbolic of the concerns of our pupils, in the hope that they will be led from the trivial and the immediate and the local to the significant, the enduring, and the universal concern.
>
> (Hull 1984, p. 13)

This strong emphasis on the need for relevance reflects an individualistic and pragmatic approach to collective worship – what matters is that each individual child is helped to develop personal ideas and views which are of direct use to them in their lives. This directly reflects trends shown in the sociological surveys concerning the broader approaches to religious belief.

Some implications of the stress on individual freedom of choice

The roots of the emphasis on individual freedom of choice go back a long way. Osborn (1995, pp. 53ff.) has argued that the Enlightenment saw the development of the ideal of the 'autonomous individual' (literally a law unto himself or herself), 'who relies upon his or her own reason to determine right and wrong'. In such an environment personal identity is found, not essentially in membership of groups, but rather through personal choices and achievements. He argues, perhaps rather sweepingly, that, 'since the Enlightenment the self has been declared sovereign; we are the creators of our own ends and purposes' (p. 94). The Chief Rabbi, Jonathan Sacks (1991, p. 42) depicts individualistic liberalism by saying that 'our moral imagination is bounded by three central themes – autonomy, equality and rights – the values that allow each of us to be whatever we choose. The central character of our moral drama . . . is the free self.' My data indicates that schools are following such a policy in their encouragement of individual pupils to determine their own belief structure. Beck (1998, p. 82) has argued that 'the requirement to make active *choices* – between competing comprehensive value systems, alternative lifestyles, different occupational possibilities, etc. – will be *inescapable* for more and more individuals . . .' Living 'the wholly unexamined life' will be 'less and less possible' and therefore children have a '*strong educational entitlement* . . . to receive an education which seeks seriously to help them to develop their potential for rational autonomy'. This individualistic, liberal approach has been strongly challenged by Sacks, who argues that 'the contradiction at the heart of individualism is that there can be a self unencumbered by tradition, unfettered in its freedom' (Sacks 1991, p. 44). Sacks emphasizes the importance of communities and tradition in the formation of the individual. One of the deeply paradoxical findings of my research was that in collective worship the tremendous emphasis on freedom of individual choice in matters of religion and world-view was counterbalanced by a strong desire to find common ground on which all could stand united.

The search for unity, common ground and inclusivity

In the maelstrom of change, which has celebrated diversity and individualism, there has also been a search for unity and common ground, both in collective worship practice and in wider society. An example of this can be found in the recent emphasis on citizenship in the UK which has found its way into both the educational world (how to nurture children in common values and commitments which can reasonably be expected in any UK citizen), and also into the debate over asylum and immigration (again, what values and commitments can reasonably be expected from anyone seeking to live in the UK). There is a real tension between those trends which lead to fragmentation, division and individuation in society, and those which seek the integrating and community-building factors in our diverse and plural world. This tension has been exemplified in the practice of collective worship in recent years. In my research sample, alongside the emphasis on individual freedom of choice, there was a central and pervasive theme of 'inclusivity' (or 'that unity thing' as one teacher put it). There was an extremely strong desire expressed by all the teachers to keep the whole school together for assembly despite the manifold beliefs of pupils and staff. Words such as 'together-ness', 'belonging' and 'sharing' were used frequently. Several teachers referred to their school as a 'community' or, less often, as a 'family', and there was real disappointment when pupils were with-drawn for any reason. There were at least two important aspects of this theme. The first is the tension between the desire to 'celebrate' the variety and diversity of faiths on the one hand and, on the other hand, the promotion of the 'Christian heritage' of Britain. The second aspect is the search for the social 'cement' which holds a school (and possibly wider society) together.

There was one feature of the observed assemblies which did give direct evidence for the desire for inclusivity – this was the use of songs and hymns. Singing only occurred in the infant and junior schools, but here there was a strong trend to using more general, non-religious hymns rather than specifically Christian ones, although the latter were still much in evidence. When religious songs were used the schools tended to use only those songs which referred to God (rather than Jesus) as these were more acceptable because the notion of 'God' could be widely interpreted across many religions and faiths. Some schools had a deliberate policy of altering hymns. One junior school, which had mostly Muslim children, had gone through the hymn book and explicitly deleted all hymns which referred to Jesus Christ as God or Lord. This approach is in sharp contrast to the attitude in the 1950s, which assumed a Christian background to assemblies, expressed in a *Times Educational Supplement* article: 'There must . . . be an unequivocal policy about hymns. They must be chosen for their scriptural soundness – woolly invocations to nature worship are not suitable – and for their literary merit *as hymns*' (*TES* 17 December 1954, p. 1175).

There were two of my interviews with no comments at all in the inclusivity category. This was very striking because all the other interviews had substantial numbers of examples of inclusivity. The most interesting exception to the overwhelming desire for inclusivity occurred in the interview with a Muslim teacher. The second major exception was that of a Roman Catholic who was chaplain in a secondary school. She, too, for different reasons, did not make any mention of the desire for inclusivity.

The Muslim teacher worked in a county (now community) school where the vast majority of pupils were Muslim. His agenda was quite different to that of the other teachers interviewed because he perceived himself to be a member of a group whose identity was threatened by the pervading liberal orthodoxy which he saw as suppressing the proper expression of Muslim identity in the school context. He was uncomfortable with the 'secular' approach of the senior management team in his school. His main concern was to achieve proper freedom of expression for all religions. He spoke at some length about the need to generate self-confidence among Muslims. This resonates with publications from Muslim educational groups. Sarwar (1994) argues for the need to affirm Muslim identity within the education system: at present there is the danger that it will be assimilated. He describes what he considers proper provision for the educational needs of Muslim children which arise from their faith and cultural heritage. Muslim groups have shown considerable unease with the requirement for collective worship. In May 1995 the Muslim Educational Trust said, 'We are increasingly coming to the view that there should be no statutory requirement for worship. In schools that choose to organise acts of collective worship, pupils should opt in, rather than opt out, by the written consent of the parents'. Sarwar (1989), writing in the immediate aftermath of the 1988 ERA, urged Muslim parents to exercise their right to withdraw children from collective worship and to campaign for Islamic collective worship. The reason given for this action was that Muslims face 'the dilemma of living within two cultures' and need to struggle 'to maintain and develop the distinct identity of their children' (p. 11). The threat of mass withdrawal of Muslim pupils was seen as a real one by those schools in my sample with mostly Muslim pupils. These schools all quickly applied for determinations and held discussions to allay the fears of parents about Christian indoctrination. Thus from the Muslim point of view the pursuit of inclusivity can act in such a way as to threaten the identity of Islam because the framework within which inclusivity is being promoted is that of liberal education and several of its implicit assumptions about the nature of religious belief are not acceptable to many Muslims. They refuse to be subsumed under the hegemonic umbrella of liberal education.

The Catholic exception was rather different. When asked directly about inclusivity the chaplain commented, 'I don't think about it actually'. This was not because it did not matter, but because she took it for granted that the school was a united community and everyone belonged. Here was a school which had an established, formalized and deeply rooted Catholic ethos. The Catholics had been accepted into the structure of the education system in a way which the relatively recently arrived Muslims have not been (although some government money and 'aided' status was granted to some Muslim schools in January 1998). They were keen to perpetuate Catholic identity, but did not have to battle against what was perceived as a hostile system. In sociologist Peter Berger's terms they were operating within their own 'plausibility structure', and within it they were very confident in their own identity (Berger and Kellner 1981, pp. 63ff.). The Catholic Church has worked hard to develop this system of schooling which they see as central to nurturing Catholic young people. The school is seen not primarily as an educational institution, but as a community of faith (see Arthur 1995, p. 57).

What is unity? The search for 'social cement'

Although there was an overwhelming desire for inclusivity there was far less explanation of what the substance of this school unity might be. In part it was a search for 'shared values' or 'common ground', but often teachers struggled to go further than this in their comments. The word 'collective' illustrates the problem. All the teachers were well aware that those gathered for assembly were often of many different faiths, views and cultural backgrounds. They were collected together for schooling, but was it only that which united them? What place, if any, did religious belief have? The desire for the unity of the school is nothing new and, in part, it derives from the need for the school institution to work coherently in order to achieve its educational goals, but the strength of this desire in the teachers suggested that there was something more powerful and fundamental at work, which went beyond the school as an institution and into the nature of society itself.

In some respects the use of school worship to build a sense of unity and common values reflects the seminal views on religion of one of the founding fathers of sociology, Emile Durkheim. Writing in the early twentieth century, he interpreted religion in a functionalist manner: it both unites people and provides a common moral base. He suggested that with the decline in traditional institutional religion, society would continue to need a functional equivalent with 'ceremonies which do not differ from religious ceremonies, either in their object, the results they produce, or the processes to be employed to attain these results' (Durkheim 1915, p. 427). Durkheim did not consider school rituals directly, but his views would seem to imply that these could have an important part to play in wider society. Bernstein et al. (1971, pp. 160ff.), in a discussion of ritual in education, spoke of 'consensual rituals' which 'function so as to bind all members of the school, staff and pupils as a moral community, as a distinct collectivity'. They made the important point that in an increasingly pluralistic society 'the response to the consensual rituals is likely to be weakened because of ambiguity in society's central value systems . . . ' The 1944 Education Act had implicitly assumed that it was Christian beliefs and values which provided the uniting factor for the nation's schools (see Souper and Kay 1983, pp. 6, 9). The wisdom and accuracy of this was doubted at the time and it has come under increasing criticism ever since given the secular, plural and postmodern trends in society.

One of the main reasons teachers found it so difficult to identify the substance of the 'inclusivity' which they so desired in the school community was the fact that there has been a process of fragmentation, individualization and relativization with regard to religious and other world-views (European Values Group 1992, pp. 5, 7). In order to achieve inclusivity most teachers adopted a tactic of celebrating the diversity of faiths which involved valuing them all equally, treating them all as 'equally valid', and promoting attitudes of respect, tolerance and mutual understanding. The teachers avoided making any evaluative comments about different faiths because they did not want to cause offence or fragmentation. This trend to celebrate diversity unequivocally was tempered by the desire of several teachers to help pupils to be aware of and to understand the Christian heritage of Britain. The European Values Study has suggested that 'no over-arching European value system exists' (European Values Group 1992, p. 7). This presents enormous problems to the teacher who is seeking to find the common ground holding everyone together in collective worship. Was there anything other than belonging to the same school which bound the pupils together?

There were several interesting attempts to find this 'social cement'. The teachers in my research sample looked in three main directions:

- an emphasis on our common humanity ('if you prick us we all bleed', as one put it)
- a focus on the common ground between faiths ('you've got to take the common ground . . . The staff who take assemblies have the broad spectrum')
- a view that there is an underlying, universal moral code to which all people should, in some way, subscribe ('all the main faiths have got a basic moral tone to them which you can actually hit on').

These three directions are linked, respectively, to three increasingly important attempts to provide a theoretical framework for school assemblies – namely citizenship education, spiritual education, and moral and values education. In all these areas there is a burgeoning literature which reflects the need to provide a more solid basis for school assemblies.

The search for a common language

As has been pointed out earlier, these issues were not nearly so severe in the more homogeneous British society of the 1950s when the Christian faith could still act as the theological basis for school worship. In today's more heterogeneous and plural society there have been a number of notable attempts to provide a new common language to underpin the activity of collective worship – in particular spirituality, citizenship and values education. A great deal has been written on each of these, but the central issue for collective worship is whether or not any of them can provide a rationale for the activity. Do they in any sense provide a common language which can embrace the aspirations and aims of collective worship? We first have to address the general question of how we are to view such attempts to find a common language. Is it like trying to persuade people to speak Esperanto, a language which nobody at present speaks and without a history or tradition? Or can such concepts provide a lingua franca, a means of providing genuine understanding between views whose 'languages' and ways of interpreting the world are very different? Or is it the last gasp of a hegemonic liberalism, desperately trying to find a vehicle by which its view of religion can continue to dominate public education for another generation?

Sacks (1991, pp. 66ff.) has drawn attention to the need in a postmodern, plural society to learn to speak two languages. He suggests that there is a deadlock between 'two conflicting views of freedom', both of which contain 'non-negotiable values'. One is the liberal who sees religion as 'an assault on personal autonomy', and the other is the traditionalist who sees liberalism as 'undermining religious authority'. He says that the way out of this situation is to be bilingual with 'a first and public language of citizenship which we have to learn if we are to live together', and 'a variety of second languages which connect us to our local framework of relationships: to family and group and the traditions that underlie them'. In a later publication he comments that

> there is a delicate interplay between our second languages of identity and our first language of common citizenship. If we recognize only the first language, we are in effect calling for the disappearance of minorities. If we insist on second languages to the exclusion of a common culture, we risk moving to a society of conflicting ghettoes . . . Jews are used to living with the tension. For the past two centuries we have negotiated an equilibrium between our Jewish and British identities. We know what it is to speak two languages, to strive to be true to our traditions while contributing to the common good. It is not easy, but it can

be done. In a plural society, the modern Jewish condition becomes the human condition *tout court*.

(Sacks 1995, pp. 119–20)

Sacks does not say much about how the first language of citizenship comes into being. Is it a matter of de facto areas of overlap between radically different world-views? Or does it derive from an all-embracing ideology of liberalism which purports to provide a framework within which competing views can live? Sacks goes to great lengths to attack what he sees as the corrosive effects of liberal individualism, but his talk of a language of citizenship seems to suggest some kind of overarching framework is being presumed – a kind of neo-liberalism. We also need to think about the scope of such a language. It is noteworthy that he calls it a 'language of citizenship', suggesting that its domain concerns those areas of public life where we need to interact with others who adopt a different faith or world-view. If that is so, then the attempt to generate a common concept of spirituality would seem doomed to failure because it properly belongs to Sacks' second language of identity. One of the most common criticisms of the idea of spirituality is that outside of particular traditions it is a vacuous concept.

The moral philosopher Alasdair MacIntyre (1988) also talks in terms of different languages in his reflections on how people of very different world-views can relate to one another in today's plural culture. He argues against the liberal individualist account of a 'socially disembodied' rationality (p. 4) and suggests that we need to recover the idea of 'a conception of rational enquiry as embodied in a tradition' (p. 7). This, of course, raises the issue of communication and understanding between traditions. He maintains that although there are distinct traditions of rationality, nevertheless communication is possible by learning a 'second first language'. To do this he says that 'one has, so to speak, to become a child all over again and learn this language – and the corresponding parts of the culture' (p. 374). His emphasis seems to be on the effort to try to get inside rival traditions in order to understand them while recognizing that any one person can only properly inhabit one tradition. He seems to veer away from trying to develop a common language. His approach begs questions about the boundaries of competing traditions of rationality. In the postmodern moment, eclecticism seems to operate successfully for many people. We need to consider the question of which tradition of rationality a typical school pupil might inhabit. It is quite likely there will be several, some of them mutually inconsistent.

Both Sacks and MacIntyre illustrate the enormous problems raised by the need for communication and common ground in a genuinely plural world in which it is recognized that different languages entail different rationalities. Easy translation is not possible because in many areas the description of reality is radically different. This would suggest that any attempt to find a common language and common spirituality for collective worship (and for wider society) is going to be extremely difficult. Indeed the frequent cry concerning both citizenship and spirituality is that they are vague, ill-defined concepts upon which no one can agree because they are all coming from different perspectives (e.g. Beck 1998, pp. 62ff., 96ff.).

Conclusion

In the period since collective worship was first made legally compulsory in 1944 there have been massive shifts in British society and especially so with regard to religious beliefs and other world-views. The relatively homogeneous Christian culture has given way to a vibrant and diverse plural culture, although the influence of Christianity has far from disappeared. There is now an extremely strong affirmation of the freedom of individuals to shape their lives as they please. This is tempered by a continuing desire to find the elusive 'social cement' which enables such a diverse culture to cohere – usually in the form of a search for common values.

The practice of collective worship has been deeply influenced by these trends. The typical school assembly of the 1950s was a watered-down church service with a hymn, a Bible reading and a prayer. Nowadays the mix is truly eclectic. The teachers who lead collective worship are in the very difficult position of having both to respect the powerful ideology of individualism and also find areas of unity for the pupils in their schools who often came from very different backgrounds and faiths. In this respect the teachers were pioneers who were discovering what might constitute the uniting factors in contemporary Britain.

CHAPTER 4

Educational Issues

Introduction

It was to be the newly qualified teacher's first class assembly next Wednesday morning and she was looking forward to it with mixed feelings. She was well prepared, with some interesting items from the children's work to include, and she hoped to provoke some real thoughtfulness on her chosen theme of caring for the environment. It was something she had been passionately interested in for a long time. However, she was much less sure about the supposed religious parts of the assembly. She had not had a religious upbringing and held no particular religious faith, although she considered herself to be, in some vague way, a spiritual person in that she thought about the deeper questions concerning how life should be lived. Her desire to go into teaching had been built, in part, on this more general concern. She always knew that the religious requirement for collective worship was there in state schools, but now she was confronted with it directly it struck her how anomalous it was. She had had very little training for this and she was having to think hard about how to include the religious aspect along with the more obviously educational elements of the assembly. She was very uncertain about how easily they fitted together.

As long ago as 1975 the educationalist John Hull was arguing that education and worship were essentially incompatible activities. Under his analysis, worship implied acceptance of beliefs, commitment and a closed attitude whereas education involved a constant critical questioning and an open approach. Most of the deep issues surrounding collective worship arise not from the appropriateness of involving children in worship in itself, but from the placing of that activity firmly within the bosom of schools, and especially state schools.

This raises many questions about the nature and purpose of the educational process itself. Is it to provide children with skills, knowledge and powers of reasoning so that they can make their way as free, independent adults in the world? To what extent should education involve nurturing children in the norms of the wider community? What are those norms in a plural culture and who is to decide? How should the ethos of a school be developed, and what place does that have in shaping children's attitudes? How should education deal with fundamental questions about the purpose of human life and how it is to be lived? Can worship have any place in a modern state education system, or should it be rigorously excluded as, for example, in the USA and France? This rapidly leads to a consideration of the role of educators. What is their influence on children, and how should it be exercised in a morally acceptable manner? How do we avoid the much-feared charge of indoctrination – the inappropriate manipulation of children into the views and mores of their educators? How do the beliefs and world-views of teachers affect what they do in practice? To begin to answer these underlying issues we must first consider some different understandings of the nature of education.

Some very different philosophies of education

A major reason for the present problems over collective worship is the lack of an agreed philosophy of education in our plural culture. The very naming of the government Department for Education and Skills might indicate that we have come to view education in a utilitarian and functional manner – perhaps because that is all we can agree on given the variety of views about what constitutes the 'good life' (i.e. how life is to be understood and lived for the best). There are some very different conceptions of the aim and content of education, and each of these has important and distinct consequences for the place of collective worship. The most helpful division of philosophies of education for our purposes is a threefold one of traditional, liberal and post-liberal. The reason for this is that the teachers in my research sample seemed to be operating mostly within the liberal understanding of education, but the voices of those from the other two viewpoints are clamouring to be heard.

Traditional philosophies of education assume an objective reality or truth. It is the task of education to make the learner aware of that truth so that they understand the world 'as it really is'. For example, in its Jewish form this philosophy is based on the understanding that God has revealed his nature and purpose through the history of Israel and, in particular, the Law of Moses. Education is not just about learning in an academic manner: it is induction into a right way of living and a proper understanding of the nature of life (i.e. as under God). This often has a communal rather than individual emphasis as described by the Chief Rabbi, Jonathan Sacks (1997, pp. 173ff.) who spoke of himself in his own education as 'being inducted into an identity and a series of moral commitments. I was becoming part of a people, its shared experiences and hopes.' He summed this up by saying that 'education is the transmission of a tradition'. This traditional view has its counterparts in Muslim and Christian forms.

Greek and Roman philosophies of education tended to emphasize discovery of truth by the human mind rather than through divine revelation. Plato's theory of education is based on his idea of the 'Form of the Good' – an objective, transcendent base of values and ultimate reality. To be educated is to assist people to 'see' this objective truth (Bowen 1974, pp. 107–10). Some modern writers argue on the basis of such a traditional view. Mitchell (1997) suggests that education based on 'transcendent values', agreed across many religions and world-views, is tenable. A similar view was expressed by Lewis (1943), and Tate (1998) argued strongly against moral relativism, stressing the importance of identifying the 'shared values' of a society and promoting these in schools.

With the Enlightenment came the shift in many areas of western culture towards a liberal philosophy of education. Previously education in the West had been dominated by the Church, and especially the doctrine of divine revelation with the Bible as the source of authoritative knowledge, and the doctrine of original sin which emphasized the flawed character of human nature and reasoning. The Enlightenment and the rise of modern science stressed empirical observation and human reason as the route to knowledge. Increasingly, western liberal education was based on the use of reason and experience rather than on biblical revelation and tradition. The aim was to produce independent, free-thinking, rational human beings, who could then make informed and reasonable decisions about matters of human life and knowledge. The ideal of liberal education was very strong in the 1960s and 1970s and is still extremely influential in schools today.

When it comes to religious education, the liberal view regards religious knowledge as suspect and not in the same category as mathematical, scientific and historical knowledge. In particular, the educationalist Paul Hirst (1974, chapter 12) argued that we can only teach about religion (i.e. describe what religious people believe and do) because there are no publicly agreed standards or tests for religious knowledge. Matters of religious commitment are a private matter for personal choice and are outside the remit of liberal education, which sees young people as autonomous decision makers using empirical observation and human reason to guide them (Sealey 1985). Sacks (1997, p. 184) provides a thought-provoking, although possibly caricaturing, illustration of the difference between a traditional and a liberal view of education. He sees the former as akin to the inheritance of 'an ancient but still magnificent building': he characterizes the latter as 'a matter of handing a child an architectural encyclopedia on the one hand, a heap of bricks on the other, and telling it to build its own house'.

With the advent of postmodernism and pluralism, this liberal philosophy of education has come under increasing attack from a number of different directions – notably Christian, Muslim and postmodern. These critiques are both powerful and increasing in number, suggesting that the liberal consensus is no longer adequate as the dominant basis for educational philosophy and there is a real need for a coherent post-liberal understanding of education. Some evangelical and other Christians were far from happy with what they saw as the pervasive and dominant ethos of liberal education that prescribed an approach to religious belief which was unacceptable to them as it implied that such beliefs could not count as genuine knowledge and effectively treated the question of the 'truth' of religious belief as insoluble in principle. The educationalist Trevor Cooling (1994), starting from his experience as a Christian and as a teacher, considered the tension between his evangelical Christian commitment and liberal secular education. He described himself as a 'critical realist' for whom his religious beliefs were 'propositional truth about God' (p. 49) and 'making statements about the nature of reality' (p. 88). He did not accept the view of liberal education which sought to consign all religious belief to the domain of private, subjective opinion in which one view was as good as another with no rational way of deciding between them. Cooling argued against an objective, neutral, liberal educational theory as the only framework for education. He stressed the importance of making the presuppositions of any educational theory more explicit. (See also Watson 1987, Thiessen 1993, Wright 1993 and Smith 1997 for Christian critiques of the assumptions of liberal education and a defence of Christian nurture and the centrality of the question of truth.)

Another very important critique of liberal education comes from the Muslim community. As there are approximately half a million Muslim children of school age in Britain this is a significant element in the debate. The general trend in the Muslim community since the 1988 Education Reform Act has been one of growing criticism of the liberal, multifaith provision and the perceived Christian bias. The Muslim critique does not rest only on the fact that the present collective worship provision can easily compromise the children's faith. There is also a deeper conflict with liberal educational ideals and the way these treat religious belief and its truth. Sarwar has argued that

> Muslims find it difficult to accept some parts of the school curriculum, not because the subjects are prohibited per se, but because their methodology of teaching is against the Guidance of Allah. The latter must be the ultimate yardstick for Muslims.   (Sarwar 1994, p. 2)

Ashraf (1997, pp. 272ff.) writes in similar vein: 'To resist the corrosive influences of the secularist worldviews that brainwash our children and create in them uncertainty about values, it is necessary for religious groups to stand together.' He argues that the common beliefs of religious groups are beliefs in:

- Transcendental Reality and the 'transcendental character of truth'
- the essence of the spiritual dimension in each human being
- certain 'eternal and fundamental values'.

Many sections of the Muslim community are not prepared to be compromised by the assumptions of liberal secular education, and are exposing these as the assumptions of one particular world-view. Central in this critique is the question of the truth of the Muslim view. They are not prepared to see Muslim beliefs treated as relative and subjective by an alien educational ideology.

A third important critique of liberal education comes from postmodern perspectives. Usher and Edwards (1994) comment that 'education itself is going through profound change in terms of purposes, content and methods. These changes are part of a process that, generally, questions the role of education as the child of the Enlightenment' (p. 3). Postmodern thought has challenged some of the basic assumptions of education, and especially the Enlightenment ideals of an overarching rationality to which all reasonable people subscribe and an objective knowledge which relegates religious belief to the realm of private opinion. This opens the door to the possibility of a multiplicity of educational philosophies all co-existing.

These critiques are extremely important and suggest that the questions of the nature of religious belief and the competing truth claims of the different religions and world-views (including liberal education) need to be explored in relation to collective worship in schools if a satisfactory policy is ever to be developed out of the present quagmire. Another important consequence is the realization that many of the issues and dichotomies which arise in the collective worship debate (e.g. education and nurture/ indoctrination, the division between knowledge and belief, the public/private values distinction) depend on the liberal paradigm for their currency. They look different when seen from other perspectives. In short, there will be no solution to the issues of collective worship in schools without a careful account of the philosophy of education which underpins the practice. It is questionable that a uniform prescription for all state schools will suffice for the future. We are in an era of recognizing the importance of diversity. As the Prime Minister's former aide Alastair Campbell has famously said, the 'bog-standard, one-size-fits-all' school is a thing of the past. Therefore we are already in an era when the educational philosophies may differ from school to school. At the present time liberal understandings of education are still the most dominant in state education, but we need to develop a framework which fully takes into account the plural character of contemporary Britain and allows genuine space for the more traditional philosophies.

The place of worship in education

In the UK, worship has been a well established part of school life, but its role is much contested. The attitude taken depends significantly on the underlying philosophy of education. The main interviews in my research indicated that the teachers' attitudes to the 'worship' aspect of collective worship were paradoxical: on the one hand worship was seen as extremely important, on the other hand it was also deeply problematic. The following quotations from infant and junior school teachers about the worship aspect give a flavour of the tensions involved for the teachers and are typical of many: 'a really necessary part of the school day . . . important . . . a very difficult area . . . problematic'; 'Worship is praising the Lord – [but] because it's a school and they're children it can't be . . . we won't necessarily be worshipping. Rightly or wrongly, it isn't as strongly worship as it should be'; 'I regard this [collective worship] as a very important time both for the collective worship side and also the assembly side because obviously they are two distinct things . . . As far as the worship is concerned I'm less comfortable with that because you can't force people to worship'. As we can see from these quotations, the main problem is caused by the requirement for worship and the apparent conflict of this with open, critical education (Webster 1995, pp. 121ff.; Hull 1975). This tension is reflected by McCreery (1993, pp. 23ff.), who describes two models for school worship – the 'religious', which requires commitment to certain beliefs; and what she calls the 'worth-ship' model which entails the celebration of shared values and the consideration of things of 'worth'. She argues that the second model is the only one appropriate for the 'non-religious' state schools because it enables everyone to participate. In a similar vein Webster (1995, pp. 111ff.) argues for an 'educational justification for worship' which

> does not compromise the integrity of the teachers and children by attributing faith to them when none is present. It takes seriously the background, interests and experiences

of pupils and respects those without religious belief, for it is not exclusive. Encouraging exploration of views rather than uncritical acceptance of them, it asks for the use of reason and imagination, feeling and thinking of a high calibre. Engaging with world religions at a thoughtful level, it fosters respect and tolerance of them.   (Webster 1995, p. 114)

In the secondary schools in my research sample the problematic element became far more pronounced: none of the county school teachers wanted the requirement of worship to be mandatory. The furthest they went in this direction was to provide a time of quiet reflection. Assemblies were useful for the purposes of community cohesion and reflection on common values, but when it came to worship in anything like a traditional sense a line was firmly drawn – this was unacceptable. The simple result was that they did not do it – at least the 'worship' part. This was partly due to practical reasons (mainly finding suitable space and time), and partly because it was considered an inappropriate activity for a variety of reasons including the undesirability of coercion, the likelihood of hypocrisy and artificiality, and that it was meaningless to most participants. One teacher, who had a Christian background herself and was in charge of collective worship at her school, put this very strongly:

I am totally opposed to any acts of collective worship on the basis that I think worship is something that can only be done by somebody in a believing community. I don't think it is true worship if you are imposing an act of worship on people, they are not actually worshipping . . . in the average school, out of a group of 200 students, there may be a handful who, if you conducted an act of worship, would actually be trying to worship, who it would be real to, and possibly no members of staff. So the whole thing then is a very artificial affair, and because of that, I think it degrades what is called worship and doesn't actually do anything to encourage students to worship. It means nothing to them . . . I really do not believe it has any value.

What she was so opposed to was the requirement for worship, not assemblies in themselves:

I think there is a value in assemblies . . . in bringing students together in large groups . . . to do community things, school community acts – like acknowledging the achievements of students. To also have something like a theme, whereby you are putting across, if you like, a moral, in inverted commas, message . . . it is much more of a celebratory thing, or a chance to just put a new, perhaps a spiritual perspective on it – spiritual in its widest sense.

This has been quoted at length because it gives an indication of the depth of feeling against the requirement for worship, especially in the secondary schools. It is interesting to note that this strength of feeling against collective worship which occurred in the interviews was not really reflected in the school policy documents, possibly because the schools did not wish to use such a vehicle for challenging the law of the land. The policies tended to deal with the problem of worship by stressing the importance of an open, individual response to what was offered – and this usually took the form of silent reflection.

The official government and Local Education Authority documents indicated that whilst there was considerable consensus on the desirability of core values and a common moral code for the nation's schools, the question of worship was much more problematic and divisive. There is a curious ambivalence and awkwardness about collective worship in the official documents. It is required for all pupils by law and yet the documents acknowledge the difficulties in meeting this requirement. It is recognized that the worship is not corporate (i.e. a body of people with similar beliefs), but collective (i.e. a gathering of people where nothing can be assumed in terms of beliefs – there may be a complete mixture). Circular 1/94 (DFE 1994, paragraph 57) says: 'Worship in schools will necessarily be of a different character from worship amongst a group with beliefs in common. The legislation reflects this difference in referring to "collective worship" rather than "corporate worship".' This ambivalence and awkwardness can be seen in the discussion of the meaning of collective worship. The primary legislation (i.e. Acts of Parliament) does not define worship. Both Circular 1/94 (paragraphs 57, 61 and 63) and the Ofsted Inspection Handbook (1995b, p. 87) have controversially tried to push this definition in the direction of a traditional understanding of theistic worship as 'veneration of a divine being' which also accords 'a special status to Jesus Christ'. These controversial directives, which many see as the result of political pressure at national level from a right-wing Conservative and Christian lobby, go against the attempts in other official documents deliberately to broaden the concept of worship in order to make it incorporate a wide variety of beliefs and attitudes, religious or otherwise. For example, the Bedfordshire *Collective Worship* booklet says:

> One way forward might be to broaden the definition of the word "worship". Worship can be defined as having to do with "worth" and "honour". It should be concerned with identifying, affirming and celebrating certain ideals and values held to be of central importance to the community which worships. This is a useful definition as it accommodates a variety of practices.
>
> (Gregory 1989, p. 4)

These problems with the concept of school worship are scarcely new. As described in Chapter 2, there has been an increasingly loud chorus concerning its problematic nature, especially since the mid-1960s. The interesting question is why it has not yet died completely. Certainly in the secondary schools worship in any traditional sense has almost died, but this is not so in the infant and junior schools. Despite the efforts of government legislation and especially the controversial Circular 1/94, the way most schools have coped with the perceived tension between worship and education has been by radically redefining worship away from the traditional understanding of 'veneration of a divine being' and towards the idea of an open quest for what is of ultimate worth and value.

Worship 'in any sort of direction'

Some teachers, especially those from the county secondary schools, would like the requirement for worship to go, but many also felt that something indefinable and intangible would be lost and the whole activity impoverished as a result of such an action. Several teachers struggled to define what precisely was meant by worship in this context, as the following comments (both from junior school teachers) reveal: 'I don't really know what worship is . . . What is worship to me is something totally different to somebody else'; 'I'm not really sure exactly what's meant by worship at the moment – my own personal confusion'. In order to deal with the problematic nature of worship in a school context many teachers and schools gave their own definition of what collective worship involved. As we have already noted, the primary legislation does not define the term; the only attempts to do so occur controversially in Circular 1/94 and the Ofsted Inspection Handbook (1995b and 1995c). It has been widely observed that collective worship is *sui generis* and therefore it lends itself to such redefinition, especially given the problems facing teachers in a plural context. Broadly speaking there were four different directions in which the teachers looked – each of which can be characterized using phrases from the interviews. In order of increasing emphasis on 'transcendence' (i.e. the assumption of the existence of a 'God' or ultimate reality beyond the immediate observable world) these were:

- an 'act of collective responsibility' which focused on moral values
- a 'corporate act of thinking' which stressed reflection and thinking on personal values, 'worth-ship' and developing a sense of awe and wonder
- an 'act of spirituality that . . . is collective', which emphasized a vague inner dimension to human life which went beyond the material
- 'a true act of worship' involving a more traditional worship of God.

Often a given individual teacher's view of assembly might contain elements of all four of these approaches. There was considerable variety concerning which element was the predominant one. I will explore them in more depth in the following two chapters. The main point to note from an educational perspective is how uneasily a traditional approach to worship sits with a liberal understanding of education and how this has led to these widespread redefinitions of worship within schools.

The influence of the teacher – the 'new sacerdotal class'

Given this context of the problematic place of worship in education, the role of the teacher who leads it becomes critical. It was clear from my data that both the content and style of an assembly are influenced very substantially by the views and attitudes of the teacher leading it. It is their judgement which is by far the most important factor in determining what is done. This 'personal leeway' and the consequent power of the teacher to decide what goes into an assembly recalls the Tory Prime Minister Benjamin Disraeli's prediction made at the time of the 1870 Education Act, which for the first time made teachers in state schools responsible for religious education rather than functionaries of the Church. When addressing Parliament Disraeli said of this change, 'You are inventing and establishing a new sacerdotal class. The schoolmaster, who will exercise their function, will exercise an extraordinary influence upon the history of England and upon the conduct of Englishmen' (quoted by Loosemore 1965, p. 339 – from *Hansard*, 3rd series, ccii, 289). This prediction is now more true than ever.

In practice, it is vital that the teacher leading the assembly feels comfortable with both its content and its format. All the teachers in my sample spoke of the influence of their own personal beliefs on the way in which they conducted assembly. Many of them were practising members of a faith (usually Christianity) and most had had a religious upbringing. All of them wanted to avoid the charge of indoctrination and were very aware that they should not abuse their position, and yet many acknowledged that what they did was deeply affected by their own basic beliefs. The only other really significant factor was the teachers' understanding of their educational role and what it was appropriate for them to do with regard to the matter of religious belief in a school context. To some extent this understanding was expressed in school policies and the various guidelines for collective worship, but the influence of these was comparatively small when seen alongside the teachers' own personal and educational beliefs.

Several teachers' comments revealed their understanding of the enormous scope they had in shaping what went on in collective worship. As one junior school teacher put it, there was 'a lot of personal leeway'. A secondary school teacher said, 'I have this philosophy that you can pick any theme out of the air and you can build something round it. I really do believe that.' This last quotation neatly sums up just how much the content of an assembly can be the construction of the individual teacher rather than a delivery of the ideas of an external tradition – religious or otherwise. The teacher is relatively free, in postmodern fashion, to pick and choose ideas from wherever he or she wills and combine them in whatever way he or she wants. The legislation notwithstanding, the declining influence of Christianity in practice as the agreed framework for school worship has meant that the spirituality of collective worship is now very susceptible to being moulded by the teachers' influence and the choices which they make about what is to be done.

It was often acknowledged that the teachers had very different personal styles of leading assemblies and this had a significant effect on what was done. For example, one headteacher said, 'I've been doing it for so long, in a way, it's become part of the way I operate . . . When I started doing this, way back a long time ago before I was a head, I found it very daunting and I did question what we were doing. It's now become part of me.' A junior school teacher commented that 'I've developed, I think, my own style . . . you've got to be yourself.' This individuality substantially affects the emphasis, religious or otherwise, in the assembly – for example, a secondary school teacher said, 'Some members of staff will actually have a prayer and it's entirely up to the person who's leading the assembly.' Another remarked that 'any number of people having the same "Thought for the week" can come up with so many different ideas within that. It really depends on your interests and knowledge.'

When preparing assemblies it tends to be the teacher's personal thoughts, ideas and experience which are the dominant factor in what is eventually done. One junior school teacher said, 'I just like to . . . keep things floating around in my mind and collecting little bits, little thoughts.' This dominance and authority of the individual teacher over any corporate tradition was further demonstrated by the way many teachers tended to use stories from holy books or elsewhere to illustrate a theme which they had already decided upon, as shown by these comments from junior school teachers: 'As time goes on you've got a store of anecdotes, stories, tales that you can elaborate and twist'; 'I've twisted it [a story], contrived it to my own needs at the time'; 'I don't care where it comes from as long as it's a good story. It's got to be illustrative. It's got to be important. It's got to be one I'm comfortable with.' A secondary school teacher remarked: 'I tend to have quite an eclectic body of information . . . and draw it all into one.'

Yet more evidence of this dominance is provided by the frequent use of weekly themes as a basis for assemblies. The origin of these themes seems to be a mixture of the religious and national calendars, events in the school and in the wider world, ideas from assembly books and websites, plus a heavy contribution from the teacher personally. They are a truly postmodern, eclectic mixture with no external authority to commend them other than the fact that they are, in some sense, sanctioned by the school which is putting these thoughts before their pupils as worthy of consideration. It is often the work of a single teacher to decide on these themes, which gives that person very considerable power over what is thought about. One primary school teacher commented: 'When I draw up the rotas I do so with a pile of assembly books and I just look through for ideas.' A secondary school teacher said: 'One of my little jobs is doing the "Thought for the week" . . . so I suppose I decide the themes.' The vast majority of these themes were of a general moral or personal development character. One secondary school policy said:

> The use of themes is intended to give real structure and purpose to the assembly programme, and to reflect the beliefs and values of the school and society in general. Although a number of the themes will be of a mainly Christian character the nature of the topics allows for other religious and non-religious stances to be acknowledged and explored. This is particularly important as the school contains students and staff from other faith backgrounds as well as those with no faith background at all.

Another secondary school policy stated that the thought for the day was 'based upon general moral values' and had 'no foundation or affiliation with any religion'. A primary school policy said that 'themes are chosen to give an opportunity for thinking about values important to the school community, for reflection, for focusing on local and national occasions and for celebrating special occasions, particularly festivals from all the world faiths.' All of these policies indicate that the only authority these themes have is that they are deemed to reflect generally accepted values in society.

Some of the infant and junior schools had quite distinctive approaches to collective worship, and often this was due to the influence of the headteacher or occasionally other (usually senior) teachers. One infant school described itself as a 'community school in celebration' and put great emphasis on celebrating the diversity of faiths within the school community. This was a particular approach which the headteacher had developed over the years. Another junior school had a weekly 'multifaith' assembly which was always led by the same experienced teacher who took great pride in the way it was done and saw it as a central part of his contribution to the school. He said, 'It's given me, in my final years of teaching, a great deal of pleasure . . . it's made my teaching much more colourful and much more meaningful to me.' In another junior school there was a very strong emphasis on not indoctrinating, and they had gone through the hymn book to ensure that the children were singing appropriate songs. In a primary school the emphasis tended to be on inculcating into the children 'good Christian values' – the headteacher here was more at home with the moral side of collective worship. In one of the secondary schools, with almost entirely Muslim pupils, the approach was clearly within the liberal mould of the senior teachers. It was this school that was determined not to root its 'thought for the day' in any religious belief or world-view. In another secondary school the issue of collective worship was effectively sidelined under the influence of the headteacher's and other teachers' attitudes, and the person responsible felt under-resourced for the task she had been given. In all these schools the approach taken by the headteacher and the senior management team had a substantial impact on the way assemblies were done. There is nothing new in the power of the headteacher to influence what goes on in collective worship. In a questionnaire survey of 79 headteachers of primary schools in Birmingham in the early 1970s, 'great variety of approach and content was found' (Brimer 1972, p. 8). This also concurs with the research of Francis (1987, pp. 161ff.) on primary schools which found that 'the impact of the headteachers' personal religious practices on the church-related character of county schools is considerable'.

A few of those interviewed mentioned their awareness of the views of their colleagues. Often this had the effect of making them cautious about the expression of belief for fear of causing offence or possibly exposing themselves to criticism for indoctrination. Sometimes there was a feeling that other colleagues put up with assemblies, but only just. One junior school teacher commented: 'Not all staff are religious, for want of a better word, and wouldn't be happy to do a religious assembly, but they all sit in and are happy for it to go ahead.' Another was concerned that she had 'a captive audience of your colleagues as well as the children'. One secondary school teacher was aware of many staff opinions which were not sympathetic to collective worship: she said, 'The staff have got various views on it as well, so I think it is difficult.' When compared with other influences this was not a large one, possibly because those staff who were not sympathetic to collective worship saw it as marginal to school life.

The official government documents acknowledge and to some extent affirm the fact that the views and attitudes of teachers are crucial in collective worship. The primary legislation gives head-teachers in community and foundation schools without a religious character the responsibility to oversee the implementation of collective worship [School Standards and Framework Act 1998, Schedule 20, Section 4(a)]. With regard to other teachers, Circular 1/94 (paragraph 141) says: 'Teachers play a crucial part in the moral and spiritual development of pupils and make a vital contribution to the ethos of the school.' The influence of the class teacher is acknowledged in the Ofsted inspection schedule (Ofsted 1995b, p. 83).

The freedom of teachers to shape collective worship made it, as one put it, 'an awesome responsibility'. Many teachers felt constrained in what they could do because of their own lack of knowledge and expertise in different religions. As one junior school teacher said: 'I do often use stories from the Bible. I'm not very good at them from elsewhere . . . I'm less familiar with them and I hate to work from notes.' Sometimes the teachers were constrained by their own uncertainties, dilemmas, and confusions. They often used qualifying words such as 'maybe', 'perhaps', 'probably', 'I suppose'. Several teachers openly admitted that they found some of the issues very difficult to handle and simply did not know what to think or do. Occasionally this was because the concepts were problematic and, in particular, there was uncertainty over the exact meaning of worship. At other times it was because the teacher was uncertain about their personal beliefs. For example: 'This is going to sound awful at my age, but I am not actually sure about my own beliefs, I think I am still trying to sort them out' (a junior school teacher); 'I have a very genuine conflict within myself about that [whether different religions and world-views point to a common truth]' (secondary school teacher). At yet other times it was because teachers had not really considered certain issues before. One experienced teacher, when asked whether she thought worship was appropriate in today's school setting replied, 'I have never, ever considered it before.' Another secondary school deputy head said: 'Now I honestly don't know. I can't say I have sat down and really thought deeply about whether we are all searching for a common truth or not. I suppose in a sense we are.' Several teachers showed that their views were developing and changing as a result of their experience in leading collective worship. This was a complex area in which many were finding their way and were prepared to learn. For example, one infant school had changed its introductory formula to prayer from 'Hands together and eyes closed' to 'Get ready for prayer'. This was the result of a visit by a Muslim father who had described prayer in the Muslim faith. Again concerning prayer, one secondary school teacher had considerable problems if it was understood in the conventional way of being addressed to a divine being, but could accept the idea of 'internal communication with ourselves, internal communication with one's sense of moral values'. He could see a situation in which the concept of prayer could be broadened to include both aspects. His experience of collective worship had led him to reconsider his understanding of prayer. These remarks reveal the teachers' understanding of the depth and complexity of the issues underlying the practice of collective worship. Many of these issues, such as that of how we deal with conflicting truth claims between religions, are unresolved questions in wider society, so it is hardly surprising that the teachers struggle with them in collective worship.

The tension between the teacher's own beliefs and a liberal educational philosophy

The teachers had a delicate balance to achieve between the influence of what one called their 'own baggage' and the requirements of the school and educational context. They faced a powerful tension in collective worship between their own beliefs and their role as educators. Given the confused, contentious and complex nature of collective worship in a plural and postmodern society this was a very difficult and subtle task. Most of the teachers seemed to be working within a liberal educational philosophy which stressed the importance of the freedom of the individual, open and critical rationality, objective knowledge, and religious belief as belonging to the 'private' domain. This was a substantial influence on the teachers' approach regardless of their own personal beliefs. In this situation they had to be concerned both for the pupils' and for their own integrity.

There was plenty of evidence in the interviews to suggest that teachers do make judgements and evaluations about different beliefs and views at a personal level. Some disagreed profoundly with the Muslim attitude to women; others held agnostic or sceptical views about religious belief; others were greatly concerned about the dangers of an implicit relativist approach to belief; and yet others thought their own beliefs were in some sense the 'most true' or 'best' beliefs, not just for them personally, but generally. In certain 'private' contexts (e.g. a church meeting or a discussion with friends) these teachers would have no hesitation in declaring their views. However, in the semi-public context of collective worship they were very reluctant to do so because they felt it infringed the ethos of an open, critical, liberal education which sees religious belief as a matter for private decision because it is a disputed area with no generally agreed criteria on how to come to a rational decision. This view of education sees the school's role as making pupils aware of the range of views and the arguments for and against them, but in no way seeking to influence pupils one way or another in matters of religious belief.

The power of this liberal educational context was well illustrated by one teacher at the Catholic school who had spent many years in a county (now community) secondary school. In this latter situation he operated in a quite different manner – he could make no assumptions about the faith of the pupils and could not do anything which might be construed as nurturing. In the Catholic school he was freed from this constraint and able to operate in a manner in which his personal Christian beliefs and his professional role were not so much at odds with each other. He explained:

> It's a lot easier here simply because we are standing on a Catholic Christian platform here and the aims of the school and everything that runs through is a Christian pathway. In a more secular school, like the one I worked in for a long time, you have to be very careful about the stories that you choose and try to find the moral standpoint which is agreeable maybe to the faiths of all the people in front of you.

Many of the teachers with strong religious beliefs faced profound issues of conscience about how to handle the tension between their own beliefs and the framework of liberal education which has become normative in most schools. Most tried very hard to be even-handed and not to manipulate the pupils, and the concern to avoid indoctrination was very high. The teachers varied in how they responded to this tension. Some made a point of trying to be unbiased in their approach and would not even express their own beliefs – as one infant school teacher said, 'I try to be completely unbiased in the things I tell them about.' Others acknowledged that their beliefs were a significant underlying influence on the way they approached collective worship, but tried not to make this explicit. A few were prepared to say 'I believe . . .', but made it quite plain that this was their belief and they did not expect the children to share it or to see it as normative for all. There seemed to be three main factors which affected the teachers' approach:

- the age of the children – it was easier for older children to handle the issue of conflicting beliefs
- the evangelistic theology of the teacher – i.e. how and why they thought it appropriate to share their faith
- the prevailing educational ethos of the school with regard to the place of religious belief – how deeply imbued the liberal viewpoint was.

It is important to avoid too many generalizations in this matter because each teacher's approach was usually a complex matter in which they were balancing many competing forces. They were not always consistent in their views. Some would profess to avoid indoctrination and yet say such things as 'God loves us all' without any qualification in an assembly. There were others professing a 'neutral' attitude who seemed to have little understanding that the liberal view of education is itself deeply value-laden and that their approach effectively promoted that view.

There were at least four interesting examples of how the teachers dealt with this tension. These included:

- a young evangelical junior school teacher whose approach to this dilemma was to declare what he believed and offer it to the children for consideration and their own, free choice
- an older Christian teacher from a junior school who was deeply committed to multicultural education; he made such a good job of presenting other faiths that he said sometimes his 'conscience hurt'
- a secondary school teacher who initially thought the 1988 Education Reform Act was a call from God to more direct witness to her faith, but after much conscience-searching decided this could not be right and adopted an approach which had a moral rather than a religious emphasis
- a county (now community) secondary school teacher who had a strong religious background which emphasized the importance of mission and evangelism; he was also deeply affected by a liberal ethos of education which sought to be even-handed in the matter of religious belief, and he expressed this conflict as follows:

> I find that a considerable personal challenge – basically to reconcile some things that my upbringing says I shouldn't be reconciling in terms of common truths . . .
>
> I could not stand up in an assembly and say that this view of God is the same as that view of God and they are of equal worth. I think that is a far more complex matter – and that really is the sort of very fine line that I try to keep one side of basically.

A key phrase here is the 'very fine line'. It indicates the complexity of the situation. Most teachers find their own individual way of dealing with this. A simple formula of 'teacher neutrality' does not do justice to the subtleties and nuances of the situation.

Teachers are not just people who follow a liberal educational philosophy in a machine-like manner; nor are they naive religious enthusiasts eager to proselytize. They have a real tension to deal with and each does it in his or her own manner. Wakeman (1995) described his position as a Christian teaching in a secular secondary school as 'walking a mountain ridge between the slippery slopes of preaching and moral neutrality'. His approach involved giving his viewpoint as a Christian and encouraging pupils to make evaluations, but, as his analogy implies, this is a difficult line to keep.

Hulmes (1979) argued that the teachers' commitments inevitably affected the way they taught and suggested that the so-called 'neutrality' of teachers could lead to a relativistic understanding of religious belief and also to an indifference – it simply does not matter which religious beliefs someone holds. He suggested that the teachers' own commitments should be used openly as a resource in RE and that this approach avoided unnecessary and misleading pretence. In a similar vein the theologian Lesslie Newbigin (1982) argued against the standpoint of the 1975 Birmingham Agreed Syllabus which, he said, 'insists that religions are not to be studied with the idea that one is superior to the rest, but "objectively and for their own sake"' (p. 99). Newbigin concluded that:

> The central matter is surely the commitment of the teacher. We must reject the illusion of non-commitment. Every teacher is committed to something . . . He should not be asked to pretend that he is above all commitment, that he has a stance above all stances from which he can 'critically' assess them all. What will ultimately be communicated to the pupils is the commitment of the teacher, and therefore this must be open and explicit.   (p. 107)

These comments, made over twenty years ago, are still relevant. Similar tensions are still faced by teachers today. As well as the desire to avoid indoctrination, the teachers expressed a need to be true to their own basic beliefs and values in the way they led collective worship. There were several comments which indicated this: 'If I didn't believe that [common truths across religions] there would be no justification for doing it at all . . . I wouldn't have any conviction in doing it' (an experienced junior school teacher); 'I think if you are doing collective worship you have got to be true to yourself' (junior school teacher); 'I've got to believe it myself, I've got to enjoy it myself . . . I would be myself whatever school I went into and be doing the same sort of thing . . . wherever I happened to be' (church junior school teacher); 'we are also very sincere when we're up on stage, intentionally so . . . I think the sincerity does come across . . . sincerity is probably the technique by which we have everybody on our side' (secondary school teacher). In the last two of these quotations the tactic used to achieve both teacher integrity and pupil integrity in a multifaith context was to look for common moral ground on which everyone can agree. All these comments indicate that there is a real need for a more open approach to be found which allows greater freedom of expression than that prescribed by the liberal ideal of teacher neutrality, whilst still promoting an open and critical spirit in pupils.

Teachers who lead collective worship – high priests of a new spirituality?

During the debates on the 1870 Education Act Benjamin Disraeli labelled teachers as 'a new sacerdotal class' as a result of the responsibility which they were henceforth assuming for teaching religion in schools – the first time such a task had been given to a functionary of the State rather than to a priest or other person authorized by the Church. My data has suggested that the teachers who lead the collective worship are by far the most significant influence on its content and style – they have to feel 'comfortable' with what is being done; they draw on their own experience and background for material; they are often deeply influenced by their own basic beliefs and values, not in a crude way of seeking to indoctrinate the children, but in a more subtle way in that if they are not 'comfortable' with what is being done then it will not happen. In many ways they are a twenty-first-century manifestation of Disraeli's prediction. They are the high priests of the new spirituality being formed in contemporary collective worship, which in many ways reflects trends in spirituality in wider society. Teachers have considerable power to define common spirituality in an age where most pupils have little or no link with any institutional religion. The particular choices made by teachers are going to have a substantial effect on the pupils. The new 'spirituality' of collective worship is being fashioned by the choices of the teachers and each one makes his or her choice by his or her own lights. This is in marked contrast to the approach of the post-war years when Christianity was assumed to provide the basic framework for school worship. Loosemore (1965, p. 340) quoted from the 1954 report of the Institute of Christian Education which said,

> We perceive no tendency to foster 'a school religion', impoverished in itself and mischievous in so far as it might offer a substitute for worship in the churches. On the contrary, school services often draw upon the wealth of all the churches in the hymns and prayers they use.

In the vacuum created by the demise of the influence of Christianity in school worship in the intervening years my data suggests that teachers are currently in a position where they can and do create their own 'school religion' – although 'school spirituality' would be a more accurate term to describe this multi-faceted and heterogeneous phenomenon. The picture of religious belief which is portrayed in both RE and in collective worship is open to considerable distortion (seen from the point of view of the believer) if the teacher has a very large amount of freedom to select material and present it as he or she wishes.

In such a situation the pupils are highly vulnerable, especially given the widespread uncertainty and ignorance of religious belief. The possibilities of moulding and manipulation are obvious. Lewis (1943) warned that the loss of belief in objectivity leads educationally to attitudes inculcated in the young being the arbitrary decisions of their educators. The widespread belief among the teachers in my sample in common moral values and a common core to all religions would suggest that this danger of which Lewis warned is not so immediate – certainly in the domain of moral education. However, we should remember that my sample teachers mostly had a religious upbringing and many of their views were a legacy of that. We cannot be so confident that the next generation of teachers, many of whom will not have had such an upbringing, will still adhere to these beliefs. There were already trends in my data in a more postmodern direction with regard to religious beliefs, with comments such as that made by a primary school teacher, 'if you believe it then it is true'. As far as religious beliefs and world-views go, you can simply make your own reality and truth. The overriding influence of the teacher in the content and style of collective worship has substantial implications for seeing religious and other world-views as individually chosen and constructed. The general approach of the teachers, which usually attempted to be even-handed and non-evaluative between faiths, can create an atmosphere in which religious beliefs are seen as a matter of arbitrary choice with each individual taking the components he or she needs to construct a world-view which suits them. There is every possibility that this trend will continue to grow.

Liberal education – an insufficient framework for a plural society?

In the years following the 1944 Education Act it was assumed that Christianity provided the basis for collective worship in schools. Most school worship was strongly Christian in format and the authority for what it contained came from the Christian faith – it was not the construction of the teachers who delivered the worship. Today's situation, despite the privileged place of the Christian faith in the current legislation, is very different. The advent of a more plural and diverse society has meant that there are many groups with a legitimate claim to have an influence over what goes on in collective worship. These include parents, pupils, teachers, governors, faith communities, the government and society at large. The problem, in a situation of increasingly diverse views, is how the demands of these groups should be accommodated.

There is a real issue of power underlying this – if there is an ideological vacuum then the obvious danger is that the most powerful and well organized group gets its way. Teachers who lead collective worship have to negotiate their way in between all these diverse interest groups. In the context of a plural culture with no one dominant world-view, teachers have to assume the role of the arbiter of what goes on. In a discussion of educational policy in pluralist democracies, Holmes (1992) has pointed out that:

> Pluralist democracies face a serious problem in preparing their systems of education for the new world of heterogeneity

and dissent . . . No English-speaking democracy . . . has until recently had to face the combined challenges of fundamental dissent about ideology and purpose, and social, religious and cultural heterogeneity represented by pluralism and multiculturalism.   (Holmes 1992, p. vi)

Holmes suggests that

the idea of the public school in the western world is premised on an assumption of a living community sharing consensual educational goals . . . That ideal of the common school has run headlong into the realities of the modern age . . . Of all the realities, the most evident is dissent.   (p. 15)

Pluralism implies that there are genuinely competing world-views and educational philosophies. The liberal, secular perspective on education, which has dominated western schools for so long, is now being seriously challenged. Holmes sums up the nature of this conflict, in this example between traditional Christian and liberal secular views of education, when he says:

If Christianity represents truth, its exclusion from the greater part of education is unthinkable. Its truth is so central to the good life (the prime purpose of education, by the Traditional philosophy), that it would make little more sense for it to be excluded from education by the Christian than for reason to be excluded by the secular liberal. (p. 89)

There is, therefore, a real battle to be fought. As British society becomes more genuinely plural and postmodern, there are substantial questions to be faced as to what extent schooling should be differentiated for different children, who should make such choices, and by what criteria (p. 2).

There was much evidence in my data to show that the ideological framework of liberal education was the most influential one with my sample of teachers. Many of them would have been trained in the 1960s and 1970s when the views of Hirst (e.g. 1974) were dominant. This approach consigns religious belief to the 'private' domain and suggests that the school's role is simply to make children aware of the range of disputed views and leave them to make their own choices. Ideas of nurturing in a faith are firmly expunged from the common school. Such a view tends to lead to an understanding of religious belief which is relative, plural and instrumental. However, there are now many voices challenging the hegemonic position of this liberal view of education. In particular, we should note the criticism that this view itself is deeply value-laden, non-neutral, and not accepted by all. Liberalism which stressed freedom of belief turns out to be profoundly illiberal in some directions. For example, it cannot accommodate a view (such as the traditional Muslim understanding of education) which sees nurture as fundamental to education. Therefore it can be argued that it is no longer adequate as the ideological basis for education in a genuinely plural society. A more realistic approach would be to give greater recognition to the diversity of educational philosophies, of which the liberal view is but one, and create schools of a more diverse character, each based on a particular view. I will explore this in more depth in the final chapter.

Conclusion

My data has suggested that the teachers' influence is by far the most powerful in determining the content and style of collective worship, and that they do this largely within a liberal philosophy of education which is now disputed from many different directions. This influence has become even stronger with the declining place of Christianity and the advent of a plural society. Despite the intentions of the 1988 Education Reform Act, in the absence of an overriding belief or value system which is broadly accepted by all, the teachers have been put in the position of having to be the arbiters of what happens – their judgement is the critical factor. This powerful position of the teachers in collective worship has been enhanced by the official government endorsement of schools generating their own ethos and values. The way in which teachers use this influence in their leading of collective worship has a significant effect on the understanding of religious belief that is portrayed. This puts teachers in an invidious position. What is needed is a clearer exposition of the underlying educational ethos and philosophy of each school so that the place of collective worship and the role of the teacher is properly and openly understood.

CHAPTER FIVE

Ethical Issues

Introduction

There has been a nasty incident of bullying in Year 8 in a large secondary school in a Midlands town. The Head of Year is worried. There have been several such episodes recently and she does not want it to get out of hand. Such behaviour is, as far as she is concerned, completely unacceptable. She decides that the best way to tackle the issue generally is through an assembly and so she sets to work to consider how to get the message across in the most effective way. She feels very comfortable about using assembly in this way. After all, several government documents exhort schools to promote explicitly their values and ethos, and collective worship is seen as a key means by which to do this. She also knew that the Ofsted inspection framework requires inspectors to look at how well the school teaches 'the principles which separate right from wrong' (Ofsted 1995b, p. 84). Bullying was most definitely on the wrong side of the line and this was made very clear in the school's anti-bullying policy. She was certainly much happier talking about behaviour and moral values in collective worship than about various religious beliefs. There was a multitude of such beliefs and much disagreement about them, but in the area of what kind of behaviour was acceptable there was a substantial consensus amongst staff and pupils alike. This thought had led her over the years to focus most of her assemblies on moral issues rather than on matters of religious faith and belief.

The vast majority of assemblies, particularly in secondary schools, have a moral tone to them. They are aimed at encouraging pupils to think about the way they behave and live their lives, not only within the confines of the school community, but in wider society. The moral emphasis of assemblies is the tip of an iceberg. Beneath the surface are many ethical issues which need to be looked at if we are to understand what is going on in collective worship today. The ethical and moral questions which are intertwined with collective worship, broadly speaking, fall into two categories:

1 The issue of what common values there might be in either a school or wider society, and what the basis and authority of these values is in our plural world. A particularly important aspect of this is what is a morally appropriate attitude to those with different views and values – there is much emphasis in schools on promoting attitudes of respect, tolerance and understanding.

2 The role of education and schools in nurturing children into particular ways of behaviour and attitudes to life. This is linked to the very widespread and long-standing practice of using collective worship as a vehicle for moral education and formation. It is also connected to the question of whether or not schools should promote any religious belief or any other world-view. How are we to balance the freedom of individuals to live their lives according to their own choices with the needs of society for some moral and community coherence and the role of the school in promoting such attitudes? In a nutshell, how are teachers to avoid the charge of indoctrination both with regard to the moral values and also in relation to any religious beliefs and other world-views they might be seeking to promote in collective worship?

The desire for common shared moral values

Many teachers made morality the centre of their collective worship. This was often done in the belief that there was a widely agreed moral code which it was acceptable to promote. There has been considerable discussion about how a plural and diverse culture can cohere, and what, if any, common moral norms there might be. The Roman Catholic theologian Hans Küng has been at the centre of the debate about a 'global ethic'. He has said, 'I . . . disagree with Huntington's main conclusion of an unavoidable "clash of civilizations or religions". I strongly argue and passionately work for an alternative: a dialogue of civilizations on the basis of the project of a "Global Ethic"'. He declares that 'common values, standards and attitudes are easily found in the age-old religious, ethical, philosophical traditions of humanity'. He suggests that two basic principles offer 'an ethical orientation of everyday life which is as comprehensive as it is fundamental: the basic demand, "Every human being must be treated humanely" and the Golden Rule, "What you do not wish to be done to yourself, do not do to others"' (Küng 2000). This global ethic is not a new ideology, but a minimal consensus of values, attitudes and standards which can be affirmed by most people whether of not they hold any religious beliefs. Küng argues that it should be taught in all schools as a means of overcoming the present crisis of orientation in an age of moral confusion. This is not a new idea. Back in 1943, C. S. Lewis was arguing for the existence of the 'Tao' or an objective Natural Law or Order, which can be found in all major religions (Lewis 1943). Such ideas are illustrated in many schools, particularly at primary level, which have a clear set of simple rules of the behaviour which is expected of all pupils. Such rules are often posted up in prominent positions around the school building and constantly reinforced by exhortation in assembly and punishment for infringement. But the very existence and popularity of such codes of behaviour begs the question of their origin and authority. Are they simply something which begins and ends with the school community? Or are they rooted in a more widespread moral code in society?

A national debate on moral values was launched in 1996 by the then School Curriculum and Assessment Authority (SCAA) in an attempt to give schools a basis on which to develop their ethos and shared values (National Forum 1996). This was a practical exercise to discover which values were agreed upon as a matter of fact. It did not seek to make any comments about their origin or by what authority they received their sanction, recognizing that there would be wide variation of beliefs in this area. A broad spectrum of interested parties covering educationalists, politicians, faith communities and others came up with a statement of agreed values in October 1997. This had been preceded by calls by the Archbishop of Canterbury (House of Lords, 5 July 1996) and Mrs Frances Lawrence (*The Times* 21 October 1996) for an agreement on basic moral values to be upheld in the country. There has been a steady and growing literature concerning values and moral education (e.g. Beck 1998; Shepherd 1998; Taylor 1998; Inter Faith Network 1997; Halstead and Taylor 1996; Ainsworth and Brown 1995). Many regard this as a helpful way forward because in the area of moral values there is at least this widespread de facto agreement. The interesting questions are what authority such values have if they are shorn of their roots, and whether or not these values will persist. They might be seen as having a certain democratic authority. But to argue that something is morally right because the majority of people think it is so is clearly to be on weak ground, and many would want to place moral authority on stronger ground – either secular (e.g. utilitarianism) or religious. The SCAA values can also be criticized on the ground that they represent a least common denominator approach and will never be sufficient to provide a moral basis for living other than minimal public values necessary to hold society together. What is clear, however, is the widespread desire for a common moral code.

A common ethical code across all beliefs?
'The principles of mankind'

Among my sample of teachers there often seemed to be an assumption that there was a commonly agreed code of behaviour – the 'principles of mankind' as one junior school teacher put it – which could be talked about in assembly. This moral code had two main characteristics for my sample teachers. First, it was something which cut right across the religions (and therefore was much easier to handle in the context of assembly than religious beliefs which seemed so different and divisive at times); second, it was absolute and non-negotiable.

Several comments, which are typical of many from the interviews, illustrate the belief that a common moral code exists across all religions and beliefs: 'the way we behave is the same in lots of religions, isn't it? We all aim to be kind to each other, to look after each other, to respect each other, not to be horrible and nasty, to live together' (an infant school teacher); 'the different values that we have are very much alike. Everybody has got the same sort of values' (junior school teacher). Another junior school teacher suggested that it was all a case of 'bringing it down basically to the major commandments'. In a similar vein a

Church of England junior school teacher spoke of 'basic, good caring principles', and of 'the principles of mankind'. She added later, 'I think all religions teach man to care for man, basically, and I think most religions teach man to care for God, and beyond that, I think, I wouldn't go'. Another teacher at the same school talked about the 'special values we all hold', and added, 'to be a good person we have to have these values'. She said later, 'a lot of the morals are very common to all of the religions so that is something else that can be brought in as a common strand'. A Catholic secondary school teacher spoke about 'a common moral code' and commented that 'people have come to the same conclusion worldwide in these areas, therefore it must be best to deal with each other in this way . . . it's not just following one way – these people have thought this out for centuries and have come to similar conclusions.'

Many other comments illustrated the absolute, non-negotiable aspect of this moral code which the teachers considered it to have. One secondary school teacher agreed that he was trying to encourage pupils into particular ways of thinking and behaving which he described as 'ways of behaving that we see as some kind of intrinsic good'. He later expressed his view that most people believed that there is 'some kind of moral touchstone . . . that is external to themselves'. An infant school teacher described some views, e.g. racist, as 'totally unacceptable'. There seemed to be a widespread belief in a free-floating moral imperative to which all reasonable people will agree. As mentioned above, one secondary school teacher spoke of making 'non-denominational moral points'. In this view that there are certain non-negotiable norms, which it is the school's duty to establish, the teachers are reflecting a common theme in the debate on values education. Educational philosopher Terence McLaughlin (1995b, p. 25) argues that there are certain values which

> could be seriously disputed only by a person who is in some sense outside the moral realm . . . They are shared values . . . they are not matters for reasonable and civilized dispute . . . They constitute an important check on a tendency to relativistic thinking in morality.

Some find grounds for non-negotiable norms in an appeal to a higher authority – either in religious form or some moral philosophy which seeks to explain why the rules should be binding. An example of the former is Sacks (1995); the philosopher Immanuel Kant would be an example of the latter. C. S. Lewis (1943) gives an interesting defence of the existence of objective value or the 'Tao'. He argues that if we deny the existence of the 'Tao' then all value is lost and each person or group is free to fashion their own values in whatever way they wish. Educationally this means that attitudes inculcated in the young are the arbitrary decisions of their educators and education becomes propaganda. Either we accept the 'Tao' as an axiom or we allow ourselves to be driven in any arbitrary direction. The teachers in my sample did not believe that the basic moral framework they put forward was simply their own personal preference – it had an objective quality. The moral philosopher Mary Warnock (1996, pp. 45ff.) has argued that values have an 'intrinsically shared nature' because 'humans are in many important respects alike'. She challenges a totally relativist view of values which treats them as personal opinions and points to the 'very high degree of moral consensus in the case of . . . classroom virtues' (p. 51). Society, she argues, has a duty to transmit these shared values. The teachers in my sample were doing just this.

The role of the school community in nurturing moral values

Most teachers in my sample took the role of the school community as a nurturer of moral values extremely seriously and some even saw the school as a moral bulwark in an increasingly immoral society. The attempt by SCAA to provide an agreed statement of values on which teachers could base their work, and the Ofsted inspection framework which requires inspectors to look at how well the school teaches 'the principles which separate right from wrong', clearly indicate that the government wants to promote this role (Ofsted 1995b, p. 84).

Several writers have drawn attention to the importance of moral communities in the formation of moral values. We need to pay attention to the seminal views of the sociologist Emile Durkheim on the roles of both education and religion in the moral formation of the young. Writing at the beginning of the twentieth century, he argued that with the decline in institutional religion society would continue to need a functional equivalent which both united people and gave them a common moral base. He suggested that:

> This moral remaking cannot be achieved except by means of reunions, assemblies and meetings where the individuals, being closely united to one another, reaffirm in common their common sentiments; hence come ceremonies which do not differ from regular religious ceremonies, either in their object, the results which they produce, or the processes employed to attain these results.   (Durkheim 1915, p. 427)

In contemporary British society school assemblies are an important form of such ceremonies. With the substantial majority of children having no contact with any institutional religion, the role of the school as a place where common values are formed is increasingly important, although this begs the question of how effective the school is in this task when compared with other influences such as peers, family and the media.

The theologian Robin Gill (1992, p. 51) has noted that 'the purely individual, rational paradigm within which so much moral philosophy has been cast, is inadequate. To resolve moral issues adequately within society there needs to be some community or communities which share values together.' His principal argument is concerned with Christian churches and he suggests that 'worshipping communities may still be significant harbingers and carriers of values in an often fragmented world' (p. 2), but he cites the work of both MacIntyre (1988) and Bellah et al. (1985) in support of the more general conclusion that 'communities are essential for nurturing and sustaining values in society' (p. 52). He comments that 'religious and moral visions are passed on through communities. They are not simply argued out on rational principles from individual to individual. They are acquired as much through belonging' (p. 21). The writings of Sacks (1991) and Mitchell (1994) have also emphasized the importance of communities and traditions in moral formation.

The disintegration and decline of so many traditional communities (e.g. church congregations and families) and the lack of an agreed moral authority in our fragmented society often leaves the teachers in an invidious position of being both arbiters and promoters of morality. They are required to produce statements about school values and ethos and to inculcate those values into the lives of their pupils. There are clearly profound issues underlying this with regard to the status of any such values, their relationship to values derived from other sources such as religious belief, and the propriety of the promotion of such values by a school.

Collective worship as an 'act of collective responsibility'

In practice the most prevalent direction in which the teachers turned in their attempts to reshape collective worship was a moral one. Whereas talk of worship in any traditional sense caused considerable pedagogical concern, the role of promoting moral sensitivity and moulding behaviour in certain ways commanded almost universal assent. This was seen as a desirable and acceptable purpose for collective worship and was very deep-rooted across all the interviews, regardless of the age and background of pupils, the type of school, or the beliefs and views of the teacher. There were several graphic illustrations in my interviews of the centrality in collective worship of promoting moral sensitivity in pupils: 'I think we are looking at the children heightening their awareness of the power of goodness . . . I think with our mixed religions we're really looking at the power of goodness and trying to encourage the children to be aware of that, and how we can stimulate that in them' (a junior school teacher); 'I do believe that we should be encouraging social and moral behaviour' (primary school teacher); 'I would think of it more as a moral context, and an opportunity to get them to think about how they are and how they should be and how they relate to each other' (infant school teacher).

Sometimes the teachers seemed to view the school as a moral oasis in an increasingly immoral society. For example, a primary school teacher said the main aim of her assemblies was 'to teach the children good Christian values . . . particularly in a society where things are breaking down so rapidly. Quite possibly the only set of values a child meets that are reasonable values could well be those that it meets at school.' A junior school headteacher said, 'We've got to build some sort of social cohesion . . . I think it's more important than it's ever been now because we see society in so many ways breaking up . . . In the new millennium there are going to be even fewer shared rules, shared values than there are now.' One secondary school teacher spoke about assembly being an alternative influence (to the media and peer groups) on youngsters to give them different ideas about how they should live and behave. She tried, for example, to make them think about the amount of swearing which they did almost unconsciously.

All schools stressed the importance of school ethos and a very important part of this was moral behaviour. Teachers tried to encourage particular types of behaviour within the school. One church secondary school teacher commented, 'Year 9 are horrible to one another most of the time. It's the worst age group, so we try to spend quite a bit of time on that.' Another secondary school teacher described assemblies as 'the touchstone of our expectations'. He also commented on the assembly themes list, saying 'there's a very strong moral dimension to it'. He described the aim of his assembly as 'presenting working together as the morally correct thing to do' and he spoke of using holy books to make 'non-denominational moral points' which seemed to indicate a belief in a free-floating or tradition-free morality which was universal.

For some teachers the moral dimension was seen as part of what was meant by worship. One Church of England junior school teacher, when asked about the meaning of worship in the school context, included 'the idea of teaching them about the morals' in her understanding of worship. An infant school teacher described her understanding of worship as 'learning about God and telling the children about God and how we ought to behave towards each other, to appreciate each other'. This teacher had a strong Christian faith, but clearly the moral aspect of assemblies was very important. One primary school teacher was unequivocal about where the heart of his assemblies lay. He described his aims as 'getting across to the children en masse how to behave and how to live their lives' and 'trying to get them to realize the usual messages of being nice to each other, and being sensible'. The moral aspect was so central to this teacher's view of assembly that he wanted to describe it as 'an act of collective responsibility with certain messages coming across'.

This strong emphasis on moral development also occurred in the school policy documents. In all the county secondary schools

there was much talk of shared values. In every case this com-
monality was seen in terms of general moral values and primarily
concerned with behaviour. A guideline in one school said
emphatically that 'the *thought for the day* will be based upon
general moral values and have no foundation or affiliation with
any religion'. Another policy described assembly as 'providing a
time to expose and reflect upon common values, including moral
values'. The infant and junior school policies all saw the teaching
of moral values as central to assembly. This was usually commented
upon in Ofsted reports. The phrase 'school values' occurred
frequently, indicating that the school was effectively the arbiter
of morality, at least within its own confines. One junior school
policy spoke with great commitment about 'the absolute values
of the school'. Another infant school policy declared with almost
evangelical fervour that in assembly 'the values and ideals we
share are proclaimed'.

There is a clear sense here of the school as a moral community
whose task is to nurture children into the commonly accepted
values of that community. As we have already noted, Gill (1992),
Sacks (1991) and MacIntyre (1988) have all stressed the
importance of the community in the moral formation of the
young. Durkheim (1915) argued that religion played a crucial
role in creating the moral community and that with its demise
society would need a functional equivalent. His comments on
education indicate that he thought this could play an important
part in the moral formation of the young. Schools are one of the
few communities in present-day society which embrace all people
(or almost all). As such they are given the impossible task of not
only promoting moral values, but also deciding what those values
should be – at least in so far as they are required to declare their
shared values in their prospectuses. The difficulties of this task are
compounded by the fact that pupils not only belong to their
respective school communities – they also belong to families, peer
groups and other social bodies – and therefore the influence of the
school over pupils is only one amongst several. The problems are
also exacerbated by the very diversity of the pupils' backgrounds
in many schools, which leads to a multitude of values being
present in any given school community.

The assemblies which were observed bore out the strong trend
to focus on morality rather than worship or religious belief. The

vast majority of the county secondary school assemblies were to do with personal behaviour and attitudes, self-development or school ethos. There was virtually nothing which could be labelled worship other than some perfunctory short silences for reflection, and scarcely any direct mention of religious belief. The only noticeable difference to this was the Catholic secondary school, as one might expect. In the infant and junior school assemblies there was more apparent mention of religious belief and use of holy books. However, this was misleading because, as with the secondary schools, most of the assemblies were about behaviour and morals. The difference was that the infant and junior schools used biblical and other stories to illustrate these themes, but it was done in such a way as to be quite clear that the driving theme was the moral message rather than the biblical story. On the whole, when teachers made use of holy books in collective worship, the main thing was to find a story which illustrated the point (usually moral) which the teacher wanted to make, and the story's origin did not matter. Such an approach pays little regard to the view of holy books as intrinsically authoritative. Some comments from the interviews illustrate this very well. One junior school teacher was asked directly, 'Does it particularly matter where the story comes from as long as it illustrates the point?' She answered, 'No, I don't think so.' A secondary school teacher said her criteria for using material from the Bible was if it was 'appropriate to the theme, not just reading the Bible for reading's sake'. A junior school headteacher said: 'I don't care where it comes from as long as it's a good story. It's got to be illustrative. It's got to be important. It's got to be one that I'm comfortable with.' Similar comments are widespread in the interviews.

The official documents – shaping tomorrow's citizens via the development of school values and ethos?

My main interviews and observations of assemblies clearly suggested that schools were much more comfortable in dealing with moral issues in collective worship than with religious beliefs. In the former area it seemed to be assumed that there was a basic moral code on which most if not all people agreed, and therefore could be promoted with some confidence. In the latter area the sheer variety of deeply held beliefs was profoundly problematic to handle in the context of collective worship. There seemed to be a moral absolutism at work alongside a religious relativism. In many ways this reflected the line taken in the official government documents, which take it for granted that spiritual and moral education are a legitimate part of the schools' business. This is enshrined in the core legislation of the 1988 Education Reform Act, section 1.(2):

> The curriculum for a maintained school satisfies the requirements of this section if it is a balanced and broadly based curriculum which –
>
> (a) promotes the spiritual, moral, cultural, mental and physical development of pupils at the school and of society; and
>
> (b) prepares such pupils for the opportunities, responsibilities and experiences of adult life.

Governments have always tended to see schools as places of moral instruction, and for this to be a principal role for collective worship and religious education. In the more homogeneous society which surrounded the passing of the 1944 Education Act this was implicitly built around Christian concepts. In today's multicultural context the need for moral values is no less acute, but it is far more difficult to find a commonly agreed basis. Nevertheless, the official government documents, especially in the 1990s, indicated a determination to find one. There was a pervasive assumption, which at times seemed like a pioneering crusade, that the schools should promote certain basic values as central to their whole activity and being. There was a tremendous stress on developing a school ethos, with certain shared or core values. Circular 1/94 reminded schools of the Government's requirement to include in their prospectuses a statement of their ethos or shared values, and commented:

> The set of shared values which a school promotes . . . will make an important contribution to pupils' spiritual, moral and cultural development and should be at the heart of every school's educational and pastoral policy and practice. Every attempt should be made to publicise the school's values to parents and the local community and to win support for them.   (DFE 1994, paragraphs 2 and 3)

Discussion of 'shared values' is widespread in the government and local authority publications – notably in the important 1996 National Forum/SCAA *Consultation on Values in Education and the Community*, which suggested a de facto set of moral values which commanded wide agreement and so could serve as a basis for an individual school's moral education; and the Ofsted inspection schedule (1995b and c, section 5.3), which required inspectors to make judgements about the extent to which the school 'teaches the principles which distinguish right from wrong' – it seemed to assume that schools would know what those principles are. The mere fact that these initiatives occurred showed that some people at least thought that the pursuit of an agreed statement on moral values might be successful. Phrases such as 'socially acceptable values', 'core values', 'a basic moral template' all indicate this central concept which was very widespread in the documentation.

One particular direction taken by the official documents is the promotion of the concept of citizenship. Successive governments have tended to use schools in general, and religious education and collective worship in particular, as vehicles for moral education and the grooming of 'good' citizens. With the decline of the influence of the Christian faith and the advent of a plural and postmodern society, new ways have to be found to give a theoretical basis to this aim. Citizenship education is one such attempt. There is a growing literature in this area (e.g. Beck 1998), but whether or not it will give any more than a basis for a minimal moral consensus in a plural society remains to be seen.

Overall there is little room for doubt that both in the teachers' views and practices and in the official policy literature the moral shaping of children is seen as a central role of the school. It is assumed that there is an uncontentious core of moral values into which it is both acceptable and desirable for children to be inducted by state schools. This assumption has had profound effects on the current practice of collective worship in turning them largely into occasions for a moral message rather than traditional worship.

Should religious beliefs and other world-views be promoted in state schools?

Even if the teachers were relatively at ease with the idea of some broad moral norms which it is appropriate to endorse and encourage in the lives of children, there remains the crucial ethical issue of what other attitudes or beliefs it is acceptable to promote in an educational environment – in a word, the vexed issue of indoctrination. This has been a major fear of the teaching profession for a long time. Whilst the concept is closely allied to some less controversial ones, such as education, nurture, teaching, learning, instruction etc, the word 'indoctrination' has become a pejorative one associated with an inappropriate manipulation of malleable minds in a contentious direction determined by the indoctrinator, and it is assumed to be in some way in the indoctrinator's interests to produce such attitudes in the young (e.g. Snook 1972). Most of the teachers interviewed were very aware of the powerful and influential role which education plays in the lives of children, and of their own position as teachers and educators. They were concerned not to misuse this position of power either by limiting their pupils' freedom of choice or by abusing their personal integrity. This was particularly pertinent in the area of religious beliefs and other world-views where people take up very different stances and there is legitimate disagreement. How were the teachers to present this aspect of life in the context of collective worship so as to be true to their role as educators and also true to their own individual beliefs, and so avoid the dreaded charge of indoctrination? I shall examine how they dealt with it under three main headings:

1 the strong desire to respect the personal integrity of all involved in collective worship
2 education for choice – the idea that the role of the educator was to make pupils aware of a wider range of options by increasing their knowledge so that they can then make their own free choices
3 the tension between education, nurture and indoctrination.

Respecting personal integrity

One central way in which teachers' aversion to indoctrination of religious belief was expressed in my sample was in a very strong desire to respect personal integrity. This approach was in line with that advocated in the 1995 statement of the Churches' Joint Educational Policy Committee which was typical of many of the guidelines for collective worship issued by faith groups and others in the aftermath of the 1988 Educational Reform Act. It said that:

> The leader must neither infringe the integrity of particular believers nor appear to require hypocritical responses from pupils and staff. Sincerity and integrity are essential in the practice of worship.   (CJEPC 1995, paragraph 5.5)

This respect for personal integrity was expressed in at least three different ways: not causing unnecessary offence; avoiding hypocrisy; and encouraging mutual understanding, respect and tolerance for all people whatever their religious faith or world-view.

Teachers were very aware that they may unwittingly offend pupils' religious sensibilities through lack of detailed knowledge on their part. This caused them to be cautious in what they said and, in particular, not to make value judgements on matters of religious faith. One very experienced junior school teacher described leading collective worship in a multifaith school as 'treading on egg shells'. This theme occurred frequently and strongly throughout the interviews. Another junior school teacher summed up the views of most by saying, 'You go out of your way not to do things which would cause offence.' Interestingly, however, this theme did not appear at all in the Catholic secondary school, indicating a far greater confidence in that more homogeneous environment as to what was and was not acceptable.

Avoiding hypocrisy was a relatively weak theme in the interviews, which suggests that the schools had managed to devise ways of leading collective worship which avoided this danger. The strong emphasis of all the schools was that collective worship should be an occasion in which all could join regardless of their background or basic beliefs. Various tactics had been devised by the schools to enable this to happen, many of which have already been described – e.g. the use of more general and inclusive hymns, allowing an open response, celebrating the diversity of beliefs, the avoidance of evaluative comments about beliefs, focusing on common ground between beliefs and especially moral issues, always prefacing comments about beliefs by such phrases as 'Christians believe . . .' or 'Muslims believe . . .', and the avoidance of areas of potential conflict between beliefs. In the government documents the main provisions in the 1988 Education Reform Act for the avoidance of hypocrisy were:

- the right of withdrawal for both pupils and teachers from the act of collective worship (retained from the 1944 Education Act)
- the ability of the school to apply for a 'determination' (section 12)
- the requirement that the collective worship should take into account the family backgrounds, ages and aptitudes of the pupils [section 7.(5)].

Of these provisions (which have essentially been retained in subsequent legislation) very little use was made in my sample schools of the right of withdrawal – the main group being Jehovah's Witnesses. Ofsted reports on 'Religious Education and Collective Worship' confirm that this is the consistent trend nationally, and also that requests for determinations are still relatively small in number.

Encouraging mutual understanding, respect and tolerance was a strong theme in all the schools. This attitude was also widely represented in the government and local authority documents. Circular 1/94 says that religious education and collective worship 'have a role in promoting respect for and understanding of those with different beliefs and religious practices from their own . . . This country has a long tradition of religious freedom which should be preserved' (DFE 1994, paragraph 9). The promotion of attitudes of respect and understanding are looked for specifically in the Ofsted inspection schedule (Ofsted 1995b, p. 63). It is commended in two SCAA discussion papers on moral and spiritual development (SCAA 1995a, p. 7; 1996a, p. 8), and in many local education authority publications. Often the need for respect and tolerance for different people became not only an equal regard for people who hold different beliefs, but also an equal evaluation of those beliefs. What began as an essentially ethical policy to enable people of different beliefs to live together became effectively a viewpoint which reflected a theological pluralism that treats all beliefs as equally valid. It was often assumed that such things as respect and tolerance were unequivocally desirable and little attempt was made to analyse these concepts and to look at their consequences – e.g. that it could lead to a facile acceptance of profoundly flawed views, or an attitude of 'incurious coexistence' as the Archbishop of Canterbury has recently said.

Education for choice – the teacher as a 'catalyst'

All of the teachers interviewed bar one emphasized the importance of making children aware of the religious and cultural diversity of the world. One of the key purposes of doing this was to enhance the range of choices open to them. The teachers did not see their role as making choices for the pupils, but rather, as one teacher put it, as a 'catalyst' in the process of choosing. No one saw the school's task as promoting any particular faith; rather the school's job was to increase the children's awareness of the different faiths and belief systems so that they could make their own informed judgements at an appropriate stage. The one exception was the chaplain of the Catholic school whose agenda was heavily dominated by a desire to nurture young people in the Catholic faith.

This aim of enhancing choices was deep-rooted in the teachers' conception of the purpose of education. There seemed to be an assumption that it was possible to present information in a neutral way so that the children simply gathered this information in an unbiased way, and then made choices according to certain (rational?) criteria. This probably reflected the prevalence of a liberal philosophy of education, with an assumption of objective knowledge. It seemed that for some teachers the concept of knowledge was not problematic and it was treated in a fairly uncritical way. For example, one infant teacher said, 'I am very aware that the children don't have much knowledge and I feel it is up to us to give them the knowledge.' One secondary school teacher summed up this approach of education for increased choice as follows: 'I don't think I am responsible for the choices they make. I can help them to make the choice, I can provide information, I can tell them where to look, but I don't think it is my responsibility to tell them which way to go.'

The main emphasis in most of the teachers was on the giving of information and the extending of awareness rather than focusing on ways of making decisions between the various views. As one junior school teacher put it:

We are making children aware of different aspects of religion, not just one way . . . [Collective worship involves] being aware that there is another form of god and perhaps extending their beliefs – well, not beliefs – way of thinking . . . We are here to give the children an opportunity of learning, of being aware . . . presenting them with these things – here's your chance as it were.

The key phrase in this is 'here's your chance', which very clearly expresses the aim of the teacher to increase the range of choice open to the children. Education is about expanding horizons. This approach of education for choice was a powerful theme across all the schools. It was summed up by a secondary school teacher who said:

It's to show them the possibilities, to show them the opportunities, help them to make their own choices, it's not for me to stand there and tell them what I think; my role more is to be a catalyst and to say 'what about?' or 'have you thought about, have you considered?'

There was a very notable lack of direction about how to make these much trumpeted choices. This issue was not addressed in collective worship. The most commonly used word was 'reflection' – children were simply encouraged to 'reflect' on the issues placed before them with no explanation as to what such a process might involve. It was a term which was virtually undefined by the teachers – perhaps as a way of avoiding giving guidance on how to make choices in these contentious areas. This may be because it is better handled in the context of a religious education class, or it may be because teachers thought that the making of these choices is a personal matter and to give guidance on how to do this might imply that some choices were better than others or it might impair the pupil's freedom of choice. It seemed that the right to make your own choices in this area was paramount, and any considerations about the rightness or desirability of those choices was secondary.

There are many places where this liberal ideal of education for individual choice is described and explained. For example, the educationalist John Hull (1984, p. 14) suggests that worship in LEA schools should be abandoned 'because this worship tries to do what it cannot and ought not try to do, and because it is failing to fulfil an educational potential which it might otherwise realize' – i.e. it inhibits freedom of thought and choice. Instead he suggests that assemblies should, from time to time, be used to impart some understanding of other religions and 'the aim of these assemblies is not to secure commitment nor to profess faith but *to deepen understanding and facilitate choice*' (p. 15 – my italics). The 1985 Swann Report takes a similar view:

> One of the major aims of education should, in our view, be to broaden the horizon of *all* pupils to a greater under-standing and appreciation of the diversity of value systems and lifestyles which are now present in our society.
>
> (Swann 1985, 465)

Swann was firmly in favour of the 'phenomenological' approach to RE as

> the only means of enhancing the understanding of all pupils, from whatever religious background, of the plurality of faiths in contemporary Britain, of bringing them to an understanding of the nature of belief and the religious dimension of human existence, and of helping them to appreciate the diverse and sometimes conflicting life stances which exist and *thus enabling them to determine (and justify) their own religious position.*   (pp. 474–5 – my italics)

Sacks (1995, p. 35) reminds us that the liberal view, with its emphasis on individual choices, is by no means the only vision of education in modern society. He contrasts a traditional, community-based view with the liberal view: 'Education is no longer seen as the induction of the young into the rules and virtues of society. Rather, it has become a way of helping children make private choices as individuals'. Haldane (1990, pp. 190ff.) argues that the liberal view

> presupposes a view of society that is fundamentally indivi-dualistic. In this conception the community is no more than a voluntary association of persons and it is to individuals that all knowledge and values are attributable. Each of us must determine for ourselves the whole content of our systems and beliefs.

This view sees the role of education as equipping children with the means of acquiring 'knowledge' rather than promoting a particular world-view. He contrasts this with the 'communitarian view' which 'holds that society is more than an aggregate of individuals', and that, 'Education is essentially the transmission of understanding: of what is the case and what ought to be done'. Hirst (1990, pp. 305ff.) distinguishes between 'primitive education' (which he sees as the passing on by a group or community of whatever they consider to be 'true or valuable'), with what he calls the 'sophisticated view of education' which is 'dominated by a concern for knowledge, for truth, for reasons, distinguishing these clearly from mere belief, conjecture and subjective preference'. Hirst expresses a clear belief in what he calls 'the canons of objectivity and reason' (p. 309) – a concept which is now widely seen as a product of the Enlightenment. The answer to the ethical question as to where to draw the line between education and indoctrination will depend upon the overall philosophy of education which is being presumed – in Hirst's terms whether or not it is 'primitive' or 'sophisticated'.

Education, nurture or indoctrination?

There was a distinct tension in many of the teachers, especially those with a strong personal faith, between the desire to give an open education, which genuinely allowed the pupils to form their own free opinions and values, and the desire to nurture the children in particular ways of thinking and living. This was not simply a matter of different religious beliefs, but was concerned with basic values and attitudes to life. Some teachers were concerned that pupils should learn about the Christian tradition, including prayer and worship. Often this was expressed in a manner which suggested a nurturing approach was being adopted. One infant school teacher who was a regular churchgoer said her aim in one assembly was 'to tell the children we all have worries and that we can take our worries to God and share them'. The same teacher said a little later, 'you have to be careful you're not indoctrinating, don't you, your ideas' – illustrating precisely that she was caught between two worlds, that of her Christian faith with its presuppositions and desire for nurture, and that of her role as a county (now community) school teacher with its presuppositions of an open, critical education. Another infant school teacher illustrated a desire to nurture which some would categorize as indoctrination. She was concerned that the children should learn what it means to pray and to worship. She felt part of her aim was 'teaching them to pray and giving them an understanding of what prayer is about'. The same teacher said she could 'show the Christian children how to be a Christian'. She doubted whether she could also show the Muslim children how to be Muslims, or the Hindu children how to be Hindus, simply because of her own background.

An evangelical junior school teacher was much more open about his aim of nurturing, and yet doing it in a way which respected the children's freedom of choice. He said, 'I try to portray something of what I believe the character of God is like, something that's meaningful and useful for the children, either to educate them more as to what God is like, or something that is useful for their day to day life.' He wanted to give the children 'some kind of education in religion and faith and what it is to worship'. One of his aims in his assembly was to show the children 'that God is interested in them'. He suggested that 'the help I have gained from my Christian faith, the way that helps me with my life, . . . can be a help to the children too . . . when you've found something good, you want to pass it on.' This same teacher was very concerned also to respect the children's freedom of choice. He saw his role as offering his beliefs, and then the children could make up their own minds.

This tension between education, nurture and indoctrination was usually freely acknowledged by teachers with regard to religious belief. What was not so much acknowledged was the possibility that nurturing in the values and ethos of liberal education might be occurring because these were part of the 'taken-for-granted' assumptions of the school. Hulmes (1979, p. 35) points out that the 'refusal to accept the claims of one religion over another is not a tactful refusal to *choose*. It constitutes a choice.' The influential Schools Council Working Paper No. 36 was very clear that the assumptions of liberal education were paramount in the school situation. In a discussion of the 'Christian as RE teacher' it comments:

> Education presupposes a common basis of agreement about what constitutes knowledge and what is only an opinion.

> At the present time Christianity, in the view of the majority, falls in the second category . . . Christianity as truth no longer belongs to this common basis of agreement . . .
>
> The teacher who is a Christian will find himself involved in both education and proclamation – he is both a Christian *teacher* and a *Christian* teacher . . . In a secular education system he must stand on the side of education; his task is to educate children.   (Schools Council 1971, pp. 92–3)

Many of the school policies stressed the importance of the educational value of the assembly. Most schools had difficulty with the idea of worship for worship's sake and sought to justify it on 'educational' grounds. One secondary school policy suggested that 'assemblies should have a curricular focus by . . . being integral to the total educational experience of the child'. This emphasis on an educational justification for collective worship appeared in many writers (e.g. Gent 1989, p. 7; Hughes and Collins 1996, p. 8; editorial in *British Journal of Religious Education* 12(2), p. 67). Alves (1991, p. 174) argued that the 1988 Education Reform Act had achieved 'the establishment of religious education (including the provision of school worship) as an essentially educational activity'. The critical question is which understanding of education is being adopted – normally it was an open, liberal one.

This assumption about the nature of education and the role of the teachers as catalysts in expanding horizons and enhancing choices immediately involves them in a complex relationship with the children's home and family backgrounds. A junior school teacher from a school with mostly Muslim children spoke of her concern to 'give the children breadth of experience of religious stories, sacred writings'. She was well aware of a delicate balance to be held in this process between her role as an educator (expanding horizons) and proper respect for the children's religious background. She said:

> Most of these children their world stops around X [an area of town Y], it starts again in Pakistan . . . although you are trying to stretch the child's experience you need to be aware of the limitations.

This indicates a tension facing the teachers: on the one hand they want to expand the children's horizons, stretch their experience so as to enhance their ability to make their own free choices in matters of belief; and yet on the other hand they profess an approach which respects and takes account of the children's family background, and very often this means the children have been carefully nurtured in a particular faith. A few teachers thought they should simply support the home tradition of the child. One said, 'We are there to support the parents' values, which is what we do.' More common was the view which saw matters of belief as the prerogative of the home rather than the school. One primary school teacher expressed this by saying:

> It is up to you and your family what you eventually believe in. I am not going to tell you that you are wrong, nobody should tell you that you are wrong if that is what you believe in. I am trying to get them to say, if they believe, their faith must be first. But they should not then say that that derides every other faith, to try to allow different faiths . . . It's a matter for the child whether they believe it or not. I try to give them an open ended aspect of it.

This teacher saw his role as encouraging tolerance and respect for other beliefs by making the children more aware of the diversity of belief, but when it came to choosing what to believe it was very clearly the domain of the child and his family.

This tension between home and school values was recognized in the government and local authority documents which emphasized the importance of the children's family backgrounds, and also their ages and aptitudes. This is explicitly stated in the 1988 Education Reform Act, section 7(5). It is underlined in Circular 3/89 (paragraphs 5 and 35) and is reinforced in Circular 1/94 (paragraph 66) which says that 'any departure from the broadly Christian requirement must be justified in terms of the family backgrounds, ages and aptitudes of the pupils concerned'. The School Curriculum and Assessment Authority Discussion Paper no. 6 recognized that 'the values of school and home would at times clash, making it all the more important to develop shared values and greater affinity between school and home' (SCAA 1996a, 17). The major example of this in my sample occurred in a county secondary school which had a majority of Muslim pupils. Despite the fact that most of these pupils have a very clear belief in God, the prevailing climate was still the open, liberal one which did not assume any such beliefs.

Most teachers firmly regarded the question of faith and belief as a matter for the individual child and their family. In the school context they had a profound fear of indoctrination and were very careful in the way they conducted assembly so as to avoid such a charge, as the following quotations show: 'I feel uncomfortable because it is my belief, you see, and I am worried about indoctrination' (a junior school teacher); 'you have to be very careful that you're not trying to indoctrinate, or you're not introducing your own ideas' (junior school teacher); 'I don't want to be seen to be promoting denominations or indeed organized religion of any sort' (secondary school teacher); 'I don't think it is right to use my role in the school to basically be a propagandist . . . you shouldn't be using your captive audience to be a missionary' (secondary school teacher); 'I don't feel I am employed to preach to the children. I am a Christian, who is a teacher. I am not a teacher of Christianity, I suppose' (junior school teacher). One secondary school teacher shied away from describing views as true for fear of indoctrination. She said, 'I feel it is part of indoctrination to actually say this is the truth.' No teacher wanted to say simply, 'this is the truth.' Most opted for a formula such as 'Christians believe . . .' and were very reluctant to declare their beliefs on the grounds that merely to state this would be to exert undue influence on the children. However, some were prepared to declare their own beliefs, but usually in such a way as made no assumptions about what it might be desirable for the children to believe. For example, one junior school teacher said:

> I am quite happy to very strongly state my belief, my opinion . . . and then it's up to the children. I also feel then that there's no argument. Nobody can come and argue with me particularly that I am indoctrinating these children because obviously you hear stories about that, but merely sharing what I believe and I have found to be helpful. If they don't believe that, they don't believe that.

Several teachers had strongly held views about which faith is the 'best', but were very reluctant to say so in an assembly. One junior headteacher said, 'I sometimes, to myself only, will say, "well, my way's best anyway!" But that is to myself. You can never, ever say that. You cannot as a head have a strongly held view that says what I do is right, what you do is wrong.' Another secondary school teacher who saw Christianity as the right way would not say so in the context of assembly 'because that's my view of the truth and it's not giving people the opportunity to make their own choices. You know as a teacher . . . they do look up to you, they do respect your opinion, and I think it would be wrong. It would be me trying to influence them.' This view was not quite as consistent as it might seem. A little earlier in the interview this teacher had said, 'I try very hard to do something religious I suppose within an assembly, but try not to force it.'

Sometimes teachers would say they do not want to indoctrinate when their behaviour in assembly came very close to that. One infant teacher, who was very concerned to avoid indoctrination, nevertheless described the aim of her assembly as putting across the idea 'that God loves us and cares for us all, whoever we are, whatever we are, and He knows and loves us all'. The same teacher, when pressed about whether there were any beliefs (e.g. very racist ones) which she would say were wrong, answered, 'I think I would try and win them over, and say, "that can't be true".' There were, in other words, a certain category of beliefs, usually moral in nature, in which the children were to be nurtured or even, we might say, indoctrinated.

My evidence suggested that the teachers were generally operating within a liberal model of education which saw the freedom of the individual as a very high priority, and the giving of objective knowledge as the task of the educator so that proper choices could be made. Such a view also consigns religious belief to the private domain. Within this liberal rationalist framework indoctrination is seen as morally objectionable and as violating basic principles of rationality, freedom, and respect for the individual. However, it has been argued by Thiessen (1993) not only that the meaning of the term 'indoctrination' is very unclear, but that it also depends upon a narrow ideal of liberal education (with its associated concepts of autonomy, rationality and critical openness) stemming from the Enlightenment which is not sufficiently sensitive to the importance of the traditions in which a child is nurtured. He argues for a new ideal of liberal education which is based upon a more open recognition of underlying beliefs, and a greater variety of schools. Children can be knowingly and openly nurtured into a particular tradition whilst at the same time encouraging them to be critical of that tradition.

It has been argued extensively that the liberal view of education is itself deeply value-laden, and hence the sharp distinction between open, critical education and indoctrination is much less clear-cut than might be suggested by the comments and fears of many of the teachers in my sample. Astley (1994, p. 44) argues that we are dealing here with 'a spectrum of merging colours rather than a sharp borderline of black and white'. Education, nurture and indoctrination are overlapping rather than discrete concepts. How you see them depends, at least in part, upon your underlying philosophy of education. The various critiques of liberal education have argued, albeit in different ways, for a much more open recognition of the place of traditions, values and beliefs in education.

Conclusion

Schools, via collective worship and elsewhere, are inextricably linked with the promotion of moral values. In a plural society this begs all kinds of questions about the nature of the values which might be held in common, and how they are to be appropriately nurtured. In the delivery of collective worship teachers are at the cutting edge of this moral debate, which affects not only the school community, but wider society. The teachers who lead collective worship are, in effect, the arbiters of both the values promoted and the means used to promote them. The relationship between these presumed common moral values and religious belief is both complex and contentious, as is the question of the promotion of any particular faith or world-view (including that of liberalism) within the school context. For collective worship to have a clear rationale there needs to be a careful analysis of these issues.

CHAPTER 6

Theological and Philosophical Issues

Introduction

Christmas was coming and, as usual, there was a headache for the headteacher of [X] Junior School. As with many schools in his town, the pupils came from several different faiths. Most people loved the nativity story and the associated carols, but unfortunately for him, when seen from a multifaith perspective, these carols were amongst the most problematic of the songs which the school sang in assembly. They proclaimed in unequivocal terms the Christian belief in incarnation – that in Christ, God had come into the world in human form. That might be agreeable to Christians, but Muslims saw Jesus as only a prophet, and Jews did not believe he was the Messiah. These beliefs seemed to be in direct contradiction with one another. How could they all be true? What was to be said, or implied, in the school's collective worship about how these differing views of Jesus were to be understood? The last thing he wanted to do in the season of goodwill was to cause any unnecessary upset or offence. So, as in previous years, he opted for an approach which simply told the story and made no comments about how it was to be seen and understood other than as a generalized message of goodwill. He desperately wanted to avoid the battlefields of religious conflict about what is true.

Collective worship is an idiosyncratic conjunction of religion and education. It raises profound questions about the nature of both activities. This chapter focuses on the theological and philosophical questions which underlie the practice of collective worship. Most acute are the issues raised by religious pluralism and diversity within an educational setting. Despite the fact that

72 per cent of people put their religion down as Christian in the 2001 national census, the UK is no longer a more or less homogeneous culture which has Christianity as its predominant religion. Although the number for non-Christian faiths is relatively small (less than 6 per cent according to the 2001 national census) we are very aware of the multi-religious nature of British society, and there is also a substantial number of people who declare they have no religion – around 16 per cent. This diversity forces us to consider how we are to handle religious belief in the public arena of collective worship in state schools. One particularly sharp issue is that of conflicting truth claims. The major faiths and world-views seem to be offering very different views of reality, and in many important respects they contradict each other. How are such tensions to be understood and treated in the context of collective worship? To dig deeper into these questions we need to explore some philosophical and theological ideas.

The question of 'truth'

Of particular importance is the question of the 'truth' of religious or other world-views and how the concept of truth can be applied and analysed. There is a vast philosophical literature on this topic and all that can be done here is to produce a sketch of the main issues which are pertinent to our considerations.

There are several classical philosophical theories about the nature of truth (Schmitt 1995; Kirkham 1995; White 1970). Of these theories, three have been particularly enduring and widely discussed: these are the correspondence, the coherence, and the pragmatic theories.

- Correspondence theories argue that true statements describe 'the way the world really is', and that there is a 'correspondence' between what is said and a presumed objective reality which exists independently of the human mind (even if it is perceived through a particular cultural-linguistic lens). So, for example, a statement such as 'God is love' implies that there is some ultimate reality, 'God', whose nature or inmost character is 'love'. If God did not exist, or were God's nature other than 'love', then the statement 'God is love' would not be true. This raises questions concerning how we really know about this presumed external reality and the exact nature of the relationship of 'correspondence' between it and our statements and mental pictures of 'reality'.

- Coherence theories avoid these problems by making logical coherence rather than correspondence with 'reality' the main criterion and meaning of truth. The really important thing is that the whole system of beliefs hangs together in a logically coherent manner. So, for example, for the statement 'God is love' to be true it must cohere with other statements of the Christian belief system such as the Great Commandment that the goal of human life is to love God and to love our neighbours as ourselves. Such an approach to truth has considerable attractions in a plural world of apparently competing world-views such as faces the teachers who lead collective worship in multifaith schools. It can allow different coherent systems, which seem to contradict each other, all to be true because the criterion of truth is internal consistency within a given system. One significant problem then is how to make choices between different systems.

- Pragmatic theories focus on facts, action and experience, arguing that the concept of truth is essentially defined by the usefulness of a belief. In the early twentieth century, the philosopher William James (1908) gave classic expression to this theory of pragmatism. He argued that 'an idea is "true" so long as to believe it is profitable in our lives' (p. 75) and he stressed the importance of 'the truth's cash value in experiential terms' (p. 200). Schmitt (1995, p. 79) points out that there are two kinds of usefulness which a belief might have: 'A belief is behaviourally useful when it empowers us to satisfy our desires . . . A belief is cognitively useful when it equips us to organise, predict and explain our experience.' So, for example, the statement 'God is love' is true if it leads us to place love as the central and ultimate explanatory feature of life and we then shape our lives accordingly. Schmitt also points out that, in the end, pragmatic theories are usually formulated in a relativistic manner since whether it is useful to believe a proposition varies from one believer to another. This makes it attractive to the teacher faced with a diversity of views in a school assembly and wanting to say they are all valid and true. One primary school teacher, commenting on the biblical story of Noah's Ark, said, 'If you believe it, then it is true'. This could be taken as implying that the essential criterion of truth is the usefulness of the belief in the believer's life.

Three important underlying philosophical issues

To investigate the way in which religious belief is regarded in collective worship we need to look not only at the question of truth, but also at some of the other underlying philosophical issues, of which three dichotomies are of particular relevance.

Realism and Idealism

Realists argue that the world exists independently of human thought whereas idealists insist on the mind-dependence of reality. For an idealist our knowledge can never get beyond the ideas of the human mind to some independent reality. Most realists recognize that we do not simply see the world directly, but only via our perceptions, concepts and ideas; nevertheless, we are in touch with some external reality. The great eighteenth-century German philosopher Immanuel Kant (1929, pp. 266ff.) drew the important distinction between 'things in themselves' (which he called 'noumena') and 'things as we perceive them' (which he called 'phenomena'). The Cambridge theologian Janet Soskice (1992) argued for what she called 'Perspectivalism', which holds that the idea of 'truth' does have some objective or absolute meaning even if people approach it from different perspectives and may, as a result, have very different understandings of the nature of that 'truth'. People are seeing the 'same truth', but from different angles or perspectives. The 'world that is' informs our theories, but our understandings of it are always human concepts and constructs.

Relativism and Absolutism

Relativism is an extremely complex and nuanced concept which has been much debated in philosophy (e.g. Schmitt 1995, chapter 2), sociology (e.g. Berger and Luckmann 1966) and theology (e.g. Runzo 1986). In general, relativism argues that knowledge and truth are always relative to a particular person, community, culture, system of beliefs, cognitive framework, intellectual perspective or conceptual scheme, whereas absolutists hold that the concept of truth cannot be completely relativized. Many teachers in my sample effectively adopted a relativist approach to religious belief, at least in the context of collective worship. In a seminal article MacIntyre (1985b) argued that relativism has established that there is no neutral point from which to assess competing truth claims. Each set of beliefs has its own way of seeing the world. In particular, the criteria for assessing truth claims and rationality are embedded within each system. As a result the predicate 'true' is reduced to 'true for me/us/this community'. He goes on to argue that this does not necessarily mean that we are all imprisoned within our own particular standpoint unable to converse with others of a different view. MacIntyre's critique of relativism (and also of modernity: MacIntyre 1985a and 1988) is highly relevant to acts of collective worship in which several different religious traditions are present and where a way needs to be found of relating them to one another in a manner which does justice both to their self-understandings and the educational context.

Knowledge and belief

The discussion about knowledge and belief investigates how claims to 'knowledge' can be justified. Is there a qualitative difference between a claim to know something and a claim to believe something? Central to this debate is the issue of truth claims (Phillips Griffiths 1967; Woozley 1949, chapters 6–8). The influence of science and the empiricist tradition in philosophy have tended to act as a paradigm for 'objective knowledge'. The seventeenth-century English philosopher John Locke (1960, pp. 320ff.) drew the distinction between knowledge and belief: the former was certain and could be established via experience and the use of reason, but was limited in extent; the latter was broader in scope, but much less well established – its rationality depending on its degree of probability. This distinction was taken to its most extreme form in the mid-twentieth century by the Logical Positivist school of thought which, much influenced by the traditions of philosophical empiricism and mathematical logic, argued that only analytic (i.e. true by definition) or empirically verifiable propositions could stake any claim to knowledge.

All other areas of discourse (e.g. morality, aesthetics, religion) could make no such claims. Metaphysical claims where no reference to sense experience is possible (e.g. belief in God) are neither true nor false, but literally 'senseless' (Ayer 1936). Such language might have emotive or imperative significance for stirring your spirit or ordering your life, but it could not be considered as making meaningful, factual claims about an objective world. This view is now widely questioned with a much greater awareness of the cultural dependency of so-called 'scientific' thinking itself and with the breakdown of the liberal Enlightenment view which saw human reason as the detached, objective and agreed means by which all claims to knowledge could be tested (e.g. Polanyi 1958; MacIntyre 1988). The distinction between knowledge and belief appeared important to many of the teachers in my sample who made a clear demarcation between what they considered as matters of 'fact' (scientific or historical) and matters of 'opinion' (religious beliefs, personal and moral values). This had a substantial influence on their approach to collective worship, as we shall see later.

The nature of religious belief

There are many, radically different understandings of the nature of religious belief and, in particular, of its 'truth' (Clarke and Byrne 1993). These have been developed, in part, to deal with some of the philosophical problems outlined above. I shall now illustrate something of the range of these understandings with a view to identifying some of the approaches which may be present in the current practice of collective worship – either wittingly or unwittingly. It may also be possible that genuinely new understandings of the nature of religious belief are being created in this particular context of collective worship. The teacher facing a multifaith assembly cannot avoid the question of how we deal with competing truth claims. As Vroom (1989, p. 13) says:

> Religions claim that they know man and the world as these really are, yet they differ in their views of reality. Questions therefore arise as to how the claims to truth by the various religions are related. Are they complementary? Do they contradict or overlap one another? These questions couch a

yet more fundamental question: what, according to the religious traditions themselves, is the nature of religious knowledge? How ought we to conceive of claims to truth by religions?

The sheer variety and complexity of views on the nature of religious belief means I can only introduce some of the main approaches which are relevant to our discussion. A helpful way of doing this is to use the philosopher Peter Byrne's typology of religious belief (1995), modified to fit the context of collective worship, partly by adding insights from other related typologies (mainly Lindbeck 1984) as well as typologies of religious pluralism (e.g. D'Costa 1986; Race 1993). I have chosen Byrne's typology as my basis because it has been specifically developed to deal with issues of religious pluralism and the fact of diversity and the conflicting cognitive claims of different faiths, all of which are not far from the surface in an act of collective worship. As Byrne comments, 'judgement as to the character and meaning of these alleged conflicts has very important bearings on what interpretation and explanation we give to religion as a whole' (p. 1). Byrne's typology covers what he describes as a range of responses to the problem of diversity (which is one of the main problems facing the teacher in collective worship). These responses he calls 'naturalism, confessionalism (divided into exclusivist and inclusivist variants), pluralism, relativism and varieties of neutralism' (p. 2).

Naturalism is 'dismissive of the possibility of finding any genuine cognitive achievement in religion' (p. 2). Religion's alleged cognitive character should be reinterpreted, for example, as an expression of emotion rather than as having a genuine factual content. The theologian John Hick (1989, p. 1) calls such interpretations of religious belief 'naturalistic, or reductionist'. These views suggest that if religious belief purports to be describing 'the way the world really is' then it should be unmasked as a delusion, false, or at least as being presented in a very misleading way. To gain a true understanding of religious belief we must look at its function in the lives and minds of the believers. Leading proponents of such accounts of religious belief include Feuerbach, Freud and Durkheim. They, respectively, interpreted religious belief as projection onto the universe of ideal human qualities, buried infancy memories of one's father and the social reality of the community with its absolute claims and supporting presence. So, for example, for Feuerbach the statement 'God is love' means that someone has made love the central defining feature of their understanding of human life, and not that there is any objective reality, 'God', which exists independently of human thought. The twentieth-century Cambridge philosopher Richard Braithwaite (1971), in an article entitled *An Empiricist's View of the Nature of Religious Belief*, gives an example of a naturalist understanding of religious belief. He argues that the real meaning of religious and moral statements is to be found in their use rather than in seeing them as statements of fact about the way the world is. He concludes that religious assertions are essentially an intention to behave in a certain way and the association of this intention with a particular set of religious stories whose function is to reinforce that intention – i.e. religious stories have first and foremost a psychological function.

Confessionalism, in contrast, 'finds cognitive success in religion, but locates it solely or primarily in one confession' (Byrne 1995, p. 3). In other words, a given religion gives genuine knowledge about the way the world actually is. Its exclusive variant holds all the cognitive merit to be in one religion to the exclusion of all others; its inclusive variant allows other faiths cognitive success in the degree to which they 'at some level approach the success of the favoured faith' (p. 3). This approach was illustrated by a Christian junior school teacher who said, 'When you believe one thing is right it is difficult to use something else . . . If I was selling a car . . . if I believed that was the best car, I wouldn't try and sell them another car.' In allowing religious beliefs 'cognitive success' confessionalism is a realist account of faith which sees the question of truth as central and usually presupposes some form of correspondence theory of truth. This relates to one of the theologian, George Lindbeck's three theories of doctrine – the 'propositional-cognitive' – which sees doctrines as informative, cognitive propositions or truth claims about objective realities (Lindbeck 1984, pp. 16, 24). Many religious believers see their beliefs as giving some account of 'the way the world really is'. For example, the philosopher of religion David Pailin (1986, p. 4) says:

Faith is an assent to what is held to be fundamentally the case, it involves questions about what is true. It is a serious distortion of the character of faith to consider it can be content to see itself as merely the expression of arbitrary tastes, upbringing, prejudice or blind choice.

Cambridge theologian Brian Hebblethwaite (1988), in a defence of objective theism, describes the influence of Kantian scepticism concerning the knowledge of the objective world and how this leads to the 'death of God' school of thought and the Nietzschean view that humanity's world and values are our own creation. He also analyses the effect of the plurality of today's world in generating relativist and non-cognitive understandings of religious belief. In Hebblethwaite's view belief in an objective God is central to Christianity and the 'question of truth' is the most basic and important of all.

Pluralism is the next of Byrne's classifications. This allows 'cognitive success to a great many of the world's religious traditions' and asserts that each provides 'folk with real contact with a single transcendent focus' (Byrne 1995, p. 5). There is 'a basic cognitive equality between faiths in putting human beings in contact with this reality and enabling them to be vehicles of salvation' (p. 6). A prime example of this is the theology of John Hick (1989). He interprets religion as 'our varied human responses to a transcendent reality or realities' (p. 1). He contrasts 'naturalistic' interpretations of religion (whether sociological, psychological or phenomenological) which describe religion as a purely human activity or state of mind, with 'religious' interpretations which are centred 'upon an awareness of and response to a reality that transcends ourselves and our world' (p. 3). He comments about the latter that 'such definitions presuppose the reality of the intentional object of religious thought and experience' (p. 3). He puts forward the pluralistic hypothesis that 'the great world traditions constitute different conceptions and perceptions of, and responses to, the Real from within the different cultural ways of being human' (p. 376). Put more crudely and meta-phorically, this might be seen as the view that there are many routes up the same mountain – a view which was often expressed by the teachers in my sample.

Relativism is the next of Byrne's categories. He says:

The key feature of relativism is the granting of cognitive success to all religions by dint of making them conceptual schemas . . . which each create or constitute their own worlds. The relativist says that truth and reality are relative to the manifold conceptual schemas into which human cognition divides. Relativism thereby has a pluriform account of the nature of reality.   (Byrne 1995, p. 7)

Hick's view is to some extent a relativist one except that he allows for a concept of the 'Real-in-itself' which is beyond all the various approaches to it. Many of the teachers in my sample took the attitude that the different religious beliefs were simply different ways of seeing the world, different conceptions of reality, each with its own validity. One primary school teacher said that her Christian faith was 'the true one' for her, but she would not say it was 'the truth': rather she would 'always preach that everyone is different – we don't all support the same football team'. Such a view corresponds with Byrne's comment that

relativism depends on a form of idealism. There is no one true account of the object of cognition because that object is not independent of us as knowing subjects. The mind must make, in some substantial way, the reality it knows.
(Byrne 1995, p. 7)

This view also has affinities with Lindbeck's 'cultural-linguistic' theory of doctrine which sees doctrines as 'communally authoritative rules of discourse, attitude and action . . . comprehensive interpretive schemes, usually embodied in myths or narratives and heavily ritualised . . .' (Lindbeck 1984, p. 32). Doctrines shape the way we see and experience the world.

Relativism would also resonate with the views of the sociologists Berger and Kellner (1981, p. 63) who regard religious beliefs as different worlds of meaning – neither true nor false. They emphasize 'the *constructed* character of what human beings mean by "reality"', and suggest that 'different people find different definitions of reality plausible' and so operate within different 'plausibility structures' (p. 63). They later raise the question, 'Can one still ask about religious truth once one has recognised that religious systems too are social constructions?' (p. 86).

Neutralism is the last and most sceptical of the views of

religious belief described by Byrne (1995, p. 8). It 'refuses to say which religions correspond to reality and which not'. It affirms 'that we do not have the grounds for awarding even the most minimal cognitive success to the traditions'. It is simply not possible to make 'global judgements and comparisons as to truth and reality in this area'. Put more crudely, someone's religious belief is 'just their opinion', their private and to some degree arbitrary choice. The theological non-realism of Don Cupitt (esp. 1984), which he explored in the television series entitled *The Sea of Faith*, falls into this category. He says:

> religious beliefs should be understood not in the realist way, but rather as being more like moral convictions. They are not universal truths, but community-truths, and they guide lives rather than describe facts. They belong together in systems, and each system belongs to just one community. They express what it means to belong to that community, to share its way of life and to owe allegiance to its values . . .
>
> Our beliefs are rules of life dressed up in pictures, giving symbolic expression to our commitment to a particular community, its values, its sense of the shape and direction a human life should have – in a word, its spirituality.
>
> There are in the human world many complete and coherent spiritualities or ways of life. Their values may overlap, but as wholes they are distinct; and there can be no Archimedian point independent of them all from which they may be evaluated. For as soon as you begin to evaluate them, you have joined one of them.
>
> Thus our most fundamental beliefs have simply to be chosen. Their 'truth' is not descriptive or factual truth, but the truth about the way they work out in our lives. They are to be acted upon.   (Cupitt 1984, p. 19)

In opting for this non-realist, voluntarist and anthropocentric interpretation of religion which sees all meaning, value and truth as a human construction, and God as 'the sum of our values' rather than as 'an objectively existing superperson' (pp. 269–70), Cupitt has avoided the problem of conflicting truth claims, but leaves us no criteria by which to make any religious choices.

Byrne adds two more 'isms' to his list, both of which occurred in the teachers' understandings. First, essentialism sees religions as 'expressions of an underlying common core' (1995, p. 9). This is related to the 'Experiential-Expressive' theory of doctrine described by Lindbeck (1984). This sees doctrines as non-informative, non-discursive symbols of inner feelings or attitudes. He says, 'Different religions are diverse expressions or objectifications of a common core experience' (p. 31). Lindbeck traces such views back to the early nineteenth-century theologian Friedrich Schleiermacher, who adopted a primarily psychological approach – religion is essentially a matter of feeling (of absolute dependence) rather than intellectual assent to a set of propositions. A significant manifestation of this in collective worship is the attempt to use the idea of spirituality as a universal part of human experience.

The second of Byrne's additional categorizations is syncretism, which is 'the attempt to harmonise religious diversity by taking elements from each religion in order to create a common form of religion acceptable to all' (Byrne 1995, p. 10). In many respects, acts of collective worship were precisely of this character.

Byrne's typology was produced to help with the problems raised by the diversity and differences between religions. Many others (e.g. Wiles 1992; D'Costa 1986; Newbigin 1989) have written on the problems of religious pluralism. Race (1993) identifies three main approaches: 'exclusivism' which sees one faith as absolute and final; 'inclusivism' which sees one faith as supreme, but allows there can be truth in other faiths in so far as they agree with the supreme faith; and 'pluralism' which sees the different faiths as equally valid approaches to the one Ultimate Reality. Race adopts a pluralist position. D'Costa (1986) agrees that these are the three main paradigms, at least in Christian theology in the twentieth century, but adopts an inclusivist stance.

This brief survey of interpretations of the nature of religious belief makes no pretence to be exhaustive. Rather its purpose is to illustrate the fact that many and very different interpretations are possible. The main question is whether or not there are any particular understandings which underlie, or are reflected by, the current practice of collective worship in schools – either by design or in practice.

Different understandings of the nature of school worship

The way in which collective worship is carried out in practice entails, usually implicitly, some understanding or other of the nature of religious belief; and, as I have described, these can be very varied. What is going on in school worship can be understood in radically different ways. Educationalist Derek Webster (1990, pp. 151ff.) gives a helpful description of 'five key models which embody society's understanding of school worship'. These are:

- the 'Traditional Christian' model which sees the natural world as an expression of the creativity of God, the role of the school as nurturing children into faith and the format of worship as closely based on that of the Church
- the 'Modified Christian' model which affirms the underlying theological stance of the traditional model, but casts its worship in a modern idiom – more varied and relevant
- the 'Inter-Faith' model which 'helps world faiths to meet with sympathy so that a genuine attempt can be made to understand each other's thinking and practice' and assumes that each has some grasp of religious truth
- the 'Secularized' model which sees religion as 'one thread of living among many', as 'a matter of private belief' that has 'no authority outside its own realm', and regards reason as 'sovereign' and as the 'arbiter in all affairs'
- the 'Other Faiths' model which seeks to allow the different faiths to speak on their own terms.

After discussing the relative merits of these models and their legality after the 1988 Education Reform Act, he concludes that none of them is adequate for what he calls 'a post-Christian technological society'. He suggests that a new 'radical' approach is needed which he sees as more in keeping with the times. This model emphasizes 'search and doubt', fosters 'questioning and critical thought', accepts uncertainty and tolerates ambiguity. He says, 'there is a model for worship here which dignifies that quest whose context is not a joyous celebration of faith but a wrestling with demanding ideas . . . This is a model which is honest about that oscillation between doubt and belief faced by those who have faith and those who do not' (p. 158). Webster does not give his model a name, but we might call it the 'wrestling questing' model. The sheer variety of Webster's models shows the tumult in agreeing an adequate basis for school worship – a tumult which is reflected in my data.

The understanding of religious belief underlying the current practice of collective worship

A key question is whether or not any of Webster's models fits the patterns of school worship, because each of them entails different understandings of the nature of the 'truth' of religious belief. We also need to probe more deeply into the understanding of religious belief underlying the practice of collective worship and its implications. Hill (1990, pp. 126ff.) investigates the question of whether or not multi-faith approaches to religious studies will have the effect of encouraging either scepticism or religious relativism. In order to answer this he gives a careful analysis of different types of relativism (epistemological, conceptual, religious) and examines the various epistemologies (i.e. theories of knowledge) which might be presupposed by the multifaith approach to religious studies. He describes these as:

- '*literal-exclusive*' which suggests that religion does give 'important truth about the nature of reality', that 'only one religious system can ultimately be right about the essentials, believes it has access to that one, and assumes that it therefore only makes sense to teach that one'
- '*literal-persuasive*' which 'endorses the view that truth-claims in sentence form *are* intrinsic to religious discourse, and that in the end only one religion can ultimately be right about the minimum core description of the world', but 'recognizes that many religions claim to have that answer' and therefore the school should teach them all and encourage 'personal choice on the most reasonable grounds available'
- '*quasi-literal-inclusive*' which accepts that 'it is appropriate to seek truth in religious belief-claims', but 'draws back from the assumption that any one religion has the ultimate key to the minimum core'
- '*mythical-persuasive*' which 'sees the function of religion to be the dissemination of general ideas and heroic stories which

reduce anxiety and foster purposeful living, while taking it for granted that there are many paths to peace' and therefore individuals should be encouraged 'to make a personal choice on psychological grounds'.

It is not necessary here to evaluate either Webster's models or Hill's typology of epistemologies of religious belief. Both can provide valuable insights into the understanding of religious belief, and especially the approach to the question of its 'truth', which underlies the practice of collective worship. The data from my research suggested that in all but the Catholic school religious belief was treated as individual, personally chosen and constructed, private (and consequently marginal to public life), subjective, relative and pragmatic.

Religious belief as individual

There was a tremendous emphasis by teachers who led collective worship on the freedom of the individual. Most of them seemed to presuppose that their aim was to produce a liberal ideal of the pupil as an autonomous person guided by reason. The free-thinking, free-floating individual was central and this outweighed any sense of community identity. The latter was by no means ignored; there was great emphasis on the school community and, in many schools, on the faith backgrounds of the pupils, but this emphasis was secondary to the importance of the freedom of the individual. For example, many teachers saw it as the role of education to make children aware of the variety of faiths and lifestyles so as to enhance their freedom of choice, and this was done regardless of the fact that many children came from homes with strong community traditions. The sociologist Steve Bruce (1995, p. 134) has suggested that individualism, which he defines as 'the right to make choices' and 'the right to define reality', is the key feature in understanding the place of religion in modern society. The European Values Study (1981–90) provides significant empirical evidence on the important influences on value changes in Western Europe and says that two of the most significant are 'individualism' (a 'sharp sense of individuation' and the 'individual as key decision taker') and 'autonomy' (people acting 'according to their own divergent norms'). The approach to religious belief taken in collective worship in my sample of schools corresponds with this trend. The educationalist Terence Copley (2000, p. 135) concludes his study of *Spiritual Development in the State School* by declaring that 'a spirituality tailored to the supreme "I" seems to be dominant within the processes of education'. For Copley, 'spiritual development is a liberal western construct locked into a secular base of a multi-cultural society in which truth questions are avoided at all costs and the truth is merely what "I" conceive it to be.'

Religious belief as freely chosen and constructed

Freedom of choice for the individual was talked about far more than the pursuit of truth. This could be driven primarily by the liberal notion that freedom to choose and practise one's religion is a fundamental human right. Some religions may give true pictures of reality, or they may not, but the individual still has the right to make his or her own free choice no matter how misguided that choice might seem to others. This openness in the matter of religious belief is founded on the idea that 'reasonable' people come to different conclusions in these matters and therefore they should be a matter for personal decision because there is no rational way of deciding between competing claims.

The emphasis on freedom of choice might also suggest a postmodern rather than liberal trend. In particular, my data showed that for many teachers there was a lack of confidence in the concept of 'truth' when it came to religious belief. Some of the interview comments indicated the postmodern idea that the individual has, as Bruce (1995, p. 134) puts it, 'the right to define reality'. Put in this way it becomes an epistemological claim that the reality we know is only what we construct. As Usher and Edwards (1994, p. 28) say, 'The postmodern reminds us that we construct our world through discourse and practice and that therefore, with a different discourse and a different set of practices, things could be otherwise.' This reflects Cupitt's anthropocentric and voluntarist view of religious belief. He argues that 'all meaning and truth and value are man-made and could not be otherwise', that 'religious beliefs . . . are not universal truths, but community-truths, and they guide lives rather than describe facts', and that 'our most fundamental beliefs have simply to be chosen' (Cupitt 1984, pp. 19–20).

The European Values Study (1981–90) has suggested that freedom is 'highly rated . . . across Europe' and there is 'a searching for a pedagogy of freedom'. This is a striving towards an increased moral autonomy for individual people and a greater sense of personal identity. This pedagogy 'should seek to develop a society in which enterprise, autonomy, self-determination, and personal growth are valued'. They argue that 'the future orientation of education is likely to be influenced by values which are concerned with matters such as "enterprise", and participation in the processes of education which lead to greater autonomy for the individual and a greater sense of responsibility for their own future' (European Values Study 1992, pp. 55–6). The approach to religious belief which occurred in collective worship in my sample schools was largely in line with this 'pedagogy of freedom' with its emphasis on increasing self-definition rather than finding identity and purpose within an existing, given tradition, religious or otherwise.

Religious belief as private

All the teachers were emphatic that it was not the role of the school to favour one particular religion in the sense of regarding it as superior or more true than the others. All beliefs were to be afforded equal respect and seen as equally valid – at least as far as official school policy was regarded. This is in keeping with a simple view of liberalism which regards the State's role as establishing the conditions whereby individuals can follow their freely chosen religions – it is not the State's task to favour one or another. As Halstead (1996, p. 21) puts it:

> Typically, no one conception of the good life is favoured in liberalism, and a vast range of life-styles, commitments, priorities, occupational roles and life-plans form a marketplace of ideas within the liberal framework . . . Liberalism makes an important distinction between the private and public domains . . . Thus, for example, religion is seen as a private and voluntary matter for the individual . . .

The philosopher of education Terence McLaughlin (1995b, pp. 26–7) has provided a careful analysis of the distinction between public and private values which is so central to liberalism. He comments:

> The broad theory of liberalism draws a distinction between public and private values . . . Public values are those which, in virtue of their fundamentality or inescapability, are seen as binding on all persons. Frequently embodied in law, and expressed in terms of rights, they include such matters as basic social morality and, in democratic societies, a range of fundamental democratic principles such as freedom of speech and justice. Public values in such societies also include ideals such as personal autonomy and the maximisation of the freedom of individuals to pursue their fuller conception of the good within a framework of justice . . . The liberal project is to specify a range of public values, free from significantly controversial assumptions and judgements, which can generate principles for the conduct of relations between people who disagree [on other matters].

McLaughlin is well aware that this division is a complex and contested one, but argues that it is useful and can be justified. As far as what goes on in schools is concerned, he maintains that in the area of 'common, universal, or public matters' education should seek 'to achieve a strong, substantial influence on the beliefs of pupils and on their wider development as persons'; whilst on 'diverse, particular, or non-public matters', it should seek to achieve 'a principled forbearance of influence: it seeks not to shape either the beliefs or the personal qualities of pupils in the light of any substantial or comprehensive conception of the good which is significantly controversial'. Instead, 'education is either silent about such matters or encourages pupils to come to their own reflective decision about them' (McLaughlin 1995a, p. 241).

This description generally reflects the manner in which the teachers in my sample acted with regard to religious belief although the reality is far more complex because the teachers were deeply influenced in their approach to collective worship in many subtle and implicit ways by their own beliefs, and were not nearly so thoroughly consistent as McLaughlin's account. The teachers seemed to be operating on an assumption that the division between public and private values was a relatively straightforward matter: liberal education and the school ethos belonged to the former category and religious belief to the latter. However, the tensions which some of them were feeling in the context of collective worship illustrated that the situation is not so simple and a deeper analysis is necessary if an adequate basis for collective worship is to be found.

McLaughlin also points out that 'schools have an obligation to ensure that pupils not only become committed to the "public" values, but that they also become aware of their proper character, and, in particular, their scope' (p. 248). He is concerned that schools might, by default, be promoting a secular, relativist, view of life and an ideal of tolerance and respect which smoothes away substantial areas of disagreement between differing comprehensive theories of the good. There was considerable evidence in my sample that precisely this was occurring on a wide scale, which underlines McLaughlin's call for common schools to address the complexity of the issues in order to produce a more coherent approach (p. 252).

Religious belief as subjective

The schools in my sample all, in effect, adopted a policy which did not allow for a decision between world-views to be taken on rational grounds. There was a general assumption of an overarching rationality which had its paradigm in scientific and mathematical method (i.e. emphasized empiricism and logic) and applied in many areas of the curriculum. However, when it came to differences in world-views as expressed in collective worship, the teachers not only always avoided making evaluative comments, but also made a point of affirming the diversity, giving the impression that choices in these matters could not be made on objective grounds.

Several teachers contrasted matters of historical or scientific 'fact' with religious 'opinion'. In taking this stance they were adopting the classic liberal view as expressed by educationalist Paul Hirst (1974, pp. 173ff.) and adopted in the influential Schools Council Working Paper No. 36. This division between 'fact' and 'opinion' is deeply contested. As the moral philosopher Alasdair MacIntyre (1988, pp. 357–8) puts it:

> Facts, like telescopes and wigs for gentlemen, were a seventeenth-century invention . . . What is and was not harmless, but highly misleading, was to conceive of a realm

of facts independent of judgement or of any other form of linguistic expression.

Philosophers of science have become increasingly aware that there is no such thing as a neutral description of the 'bare facts'. All description is theory-laden. The theologian Lesslie Newbigin (1990, pp. 95ff.) has also attacked the division between facts and values as an artificial and unsatisfactory one. He comments, 'The work of historians and philosophers of science has surely shown conclusively that the attempt to draw an absolute boundary between science as what we all know, and religion as what some of us believe, is futile. Both science and religion claim to give a true account of what is the case, and both involve faith commitments.' He suggests that there is

> a very powerful educational lobby which considers it improper to teach children the Christian faith in public schools, and claims rather to offer . . . an objective and critical view of all the religious and non-religious stances for living. This programme, of course, conceals from the children's sight a whole range of assumptions on which such a critical view rests. It denies to the children the possibility of criticizing that. The facts about the world's religions can be taught because they form part of knowledge. It is a fact that people have religious beliefs. But the things religious people believe are not facts. They may not be taught because they are not knowledge but belief.   (p. 97)

Newbigin does not agree with this division between knowledge and belief. He claims:

> The Church exists as witness to certain beliefs about what is the case, about facts, not values. This view is excluded from the realm of public truth as taught to children in public schools.   (p. 98)

My point here is not to argue the pros and cons of either Newbigin's or MacIntyre's analysis, but merely to point out that the popular idea that there is 'clear water' between facts and opinions/beliefs/values is hotly contested, and yet it underpins many teachers' approaches to the issue of religious belief in the context of collective worship. Their view seems based on a form of rational liberalism, which holds to the objectivity of scientific knowledge as the paradigm for all knowing. There are many who would hold that there are substantive issues at stake between faiths and that these can be discussed on rational grounds.

Religious belief as relative

The manner in which collective worship was carried out suggested an implicit relativism. Many of the teachers were explicit about this and regarded all religions as equally valid. In some cases this was an essentially ethical viewpoint that regarded all people as worthy of equal regard and respect which had become an epistemological view concerning the equal cognitive validity of all religious beliefs. It is easy to see the attractiveness of this view in a situation of many apparently competing religious faiths where disagreements are notorious and intractable and there is no apparently neutral way of solving the problem. Religious relativism absolves the teacher from having to say any one religion is better or 'more true' than any other.

For some of the teachers this view was based on a belief that the different faiths really were alternative routes to the same final reality. John Hick is one of the best known modern theologians who has tried to develop a genuinely pluralist theology which is also realist. He builds his theology on the basis of a Kantian-type distinction between the 'Real in itself' (i.e. God or whatever is considered as ultimate reality) and the 'Real as humanly thought-and-experienced' (i.e. our perception of ultimate reality). The former is simply postulated as a presupposition of religious experience. All religious experience is then penultimate. His pluralistic hypothesis is that

> the great world faiths embody different perceptions of and conceptions of, and correspondingly different responses to, the Real from within the major variant ways of being human; and that within each of them the transformation of human existence from self-centredness to Reality-centredness is taking place. These traditions are accordingly to be regarded as alternative . . . 'ways' along which, men and women can find salvation/liberation/ultimate fulfilment.
>
> (Hick 1989, p. 240)

Space does not permit a proper critique of Hick's views other than to say that it is an extremely sophisticated pluralist, realist theology. As such it could provide a theological underpinning of the understanding of religious belief which is implicit in much collective worship. One of the major problems with this is that it is certainly not what many of the teachers actually believe themselves. Some would be horrified to think that they were effectively putting forward such unashamedly pluralist notions. The difficulty the teachers face is that the liberal paradigm within which most of them are working almost inexorably leads them in a relativist direction – to an effective presumption of relativism even if this is not intended. McLaughlin has pointed out that liberalism need not necessarily slide into relativism. He comments concerning non-public values, in which he includes religious beliefs:

> One danger which the common school must avoid is that of promoting a relativist view of such values. The view that certain issues are significantly controversial, and that they ultimately require assessment by individuals, is importantly distinct from an acceptance of relativism. Beyond noting that reasonable 'non-public' values are significantly controversial, liberalism is silent about their truth and falsity.
>
> (McLaughlin 1995a, p. 251)

However, it is one thing for a philosopher of education to point out this distinction in theory, but my data suggests that in practice the schools go down the relativist road.

Brian Hill (1990, pp. 126ff.) describes what he sees as the logical conditions necessary to prevent 'an inherent religious relativism in our presentation of religious materials' (p. 132). He suggests that this involves going beyond a 'merely descriptive knowledge of the diversity of religious faiths and practices' (p. 132) by recognizing the central place in religions of exclusive truth-claims, and by developing pupils' 'ability to weigh up such claims critically' and encouraging 'the dispositions to make an informed decision about the part, if any, which religion will play in their own lives' (p.132). He points out that 'it would be dishonest . . . to pretend that all religions are equally multi-racial and egalitarian in their messages, equally comprehensive and consistent in their intellectual systematisations, or equally ameliorative in their concern for temporal social justice. They are not' (p. 132). His solution for avoiding an inherent relativism is to follow what he calls an 'impartial exemplary' teaching strategy, which encourages critical reflection, but also allows teachers to reveal their personal beliefs if appropriate. By doing this he believes that he has given a set of guidelines which 'avoid a pre-emptive bias towards either religious relativism or religious absolutism in one's approach' (p. 135). Hill's suggestions have much to commend them, but they are directed primarily at the context of teaching religious studies. With collective worship it is much more difficult to bring out the deeply embedded nature of the conflicting truth-claims, or for teachers to profess their own beliefs without appearing to take advantage of a situation in which there is no effective dialogue between teacher and taught. The deep desire of teachers for assembly to be an inclusive occasion means that they deliberately avoid areas of conflict. This means the danger of an inherent relativism is very real in collective worship and my data suggests that it is widespread.

Religious belief as pragmatic

Many teachers seemed to suggest that what really mattered about a person's religious belief was the effects it had in their life. The key question was not, 'Is it true?', but 'Does it work?' This focus on the efficacy of religious belief can be related to the 'pragmatic' theory of truth as classically espoused, for example, by William James (1908). Many others have developed this idea that the central feature of religious beliefs is to be found in their practical effects rather than in their cognitive truth. Some see the moral effects as the most important. As already mentioned, Braithwaite (1971) argued that religious assertions are essentially an intention to act in a certain way and the association of this intention with a particular set of religious stories whose function is to reinforce the intention. Phillips (1968) argued that the criteria for evaluating the truth of a religious belief are to be found in the way it regulates the believer's life. Cupitt (1984, p. 19) argued, as detailed above, that religious beliefs 'guide lives rather than describe facts . . . Their "truth" is not descriptive or factual truth, but the truth about the way they work out in our lives. They are to be acted upon.' Others, notably Durkheim (1915, pp. 415ff.) see the community-building effect of religious belief as of great importance as well. Yet others focus on the psychological effects of belief as being central. For example, the sociologist Robert Bellah (1976) has argued that the identification of religious belief with cognitive propositions was a temporary western aberration going back to Plato; the East showed little such tendency. For Bellah a far more important role for religion is the provision of meaning and motivation for a person's life. Credal statements and metaphysical beliefs are secondary; the key is the search for self-fulfilment. There was much in my data to suggest that this pragmatic aspect of religious belief was central to many of the teachers' approaches, at least in the context of collective worship if not in their own personal beliefs. Of course, this emphasis has the great advantage that it avoids the problem of competing cognitive truth claims given that the 'truth' of a belief is found in its efficacy in an individual's life. There are at least two problems with this approach: first, how we define efficacy; and second, the question of 'effective', 'false' beliefs – e.g. someone might live a very contented life in the (mistaken) belief that they were, say, King of England. There is not room here for a proper evaluation of this pragmatic approach to religious belief other than to note that it is an important interpretation which many theologians and philosophers have sought to defend and explicate; and it plays a substantial role in the approach to religious belief which underlies collective worship in my sample of schools.

The current prevailing orthodoxy – religious belief as an individually chosen, private, practical guide to living

I suggested in Chapter 2, on the basis of a survey of the literature and the manifold guidelines on collective worship, that there was 'an emerging orthodoxy and orthopraxis in the early 1990s', which was *sui generis,* educational, inclusive of all beliefs, reflected perceived common values and school ethos, and was based on a 'worth-ship' view of collective worship. My research led to the conclusion that this orthodoxy was operating in a powerful way in all my sample schools – the only one which was significantly different was the Catholic school, but even this was much influenced by this orthodoxy.

Further analysis led to the conclusion that underlying this 'orthodoxy and orthopraxis' was a view of religious belief which sees it as *an individually chosen, private, practical guide to living.* In my data four very strong and pervasive themes emerged in the actual practice of collective worship:

- inclusivity (the desire to keep the whole school together)
- personal integrity and freedom of choice (particularly in matters of religion)
- the re-shaping of collective worship in the directions of moral exhortation, individual reflection, and personal spirituality
- the powerful influence of the teachers who led collective worship.

Each of these had particular consequences (some of which overlap) for the understanding of religious belief and its 'truth'. Inclusivity led to religious belief being treated as private (marginal to public life), subjective, and relative. Personal integrity and freedom of choice led to its being treated as individual and private, personally chosen and constructed, subjective, pragmatic and relative. The tendency to locate the heart of collective worship in moral exhortation, individual reflection and personal spirituality, and in 'worth-ship' rather than in traditional worship, led to religious belief being treated in a private, individual and relative manner, often pluralist in character. Sometimes also this led to the idea that there was a universal experiential core in religions, or that they were really disguised moral intentions reflecting a widespread belief in an absolute common moral code. The powerful influence and leeway of the individual teacher in collective worship underlined the private/public distinction, and led to the real possibility of the moulding and manipulating of the views and approaches put forward under the umbrella of collective worship – these could become the enthusiasms, prejudices and views of the teachers.

This approach to collective worship, which I have labelled the 'current orthodoxy and orthopraxis', and its consequences for the understanding of religious belief, can be seen as being built on a combination of Webster's 'interfaith' and 'secularized' models of collective worship with the former encouraging sympathy and understanding of different faiths, and the latter stressing religious belief as a matter for private, individual choice. We should note, however, that there were a small number of teachers for whom Webster's 'modified Christian' model with its emphasis on nurture was nearer the mark (Webster 1990). All of Hill's epist-emologies were present, but the main emphasis was on the 'literal persuasive', the 'quasi-literal persuasive' and the 'mythical persuasive' (Hill 1990). In terms of Byrne's typology of religious belief, the predominant types were pluralism and relativism, but examples of essentialism, syncretism, confessionalism and neutral-ism (in virtue of the avoidance of evaluative comments) were also to be found on occasion. There was little tendency to promote naturalistic interpretations of religion in the context of collective worship. This probably arose from the strong desire to promote respect and tolerance, and this often occurred at the expense of a thorough-going investigation of the 'truth' of various beliefs.

We can also see the approach to religious belief underlying collective worship as lying primarily within a liberal, rationalist framework. McLaughlin (1992, p. 240) describes this as follows:

> Central to liberalism is the phenomenon of the existence in society of diversities in belief, practice and value, to which it is seen as a response. Given fundamental disagreement about substantial or 'thick' conceptions of human good or perfection (for example, religious views which provide a comprehensive account of human life and how it should be lived), liberalism holds that no such conception can be imposed on citizens of a pluralist society or invoked to characterise and underpin the notion of the public good. What is needed for this purpose is a 'thin' conception of the good, free of significantly controversial assumptions and judgements, which maximises the freedom of citizens to pursue their diverse private conceptions of the good within a framework of justice . . . The label 'thin' here refers not to the insignificance of such values, but to their independence from substantial, particular, frameworks of belief and value.

Despite the privileged place of Christianity in the 1988 Education Reform Act (and subsequent legislation), most of the teachers did not want to be seen to be favouring Christianity in the sense of implying it is superior to other faiths and world-views. What was central was the emphasis on each individual's freedom of choice, the need for mutual respect and under-standing of diverse views, the stress on a common moral framework which allowed this diversity to live together in a harmonious manner – i.e. core liberal values or what McLaughlin describes as a 'thin' conception of the good. A multiplicity of 'private' views of the 'good life' was not only tolerated, it was seen as something to be celebrated and affirmed as adding richness and colour to life and as increasing the choices open to each individual to fashion their lives as they will.

A radical shift – from communal faith to individual spirituality

The historian Callum Brown, in his provocatively entitled book *The Death of Christian Britain* (2001, p. 196), has argued that 'the search for personal faith is now in "the New Age" of minor cults, personal development and consumer choice. The universal world-view of both Christianity and identity which prevailed until the 1950s seems impossible to recreate in any form.' He suggests that the last 50 years have seen a radical shift from a widespread consensus which centred on a shared religion, to a more atomized, individual series of viewpoints on the nature of human life and identity. The sociologist of religion Grace Davie (2000, p. 176) has described this by questioning how much of the dominant Christian memory 'is still intact in modern Europe'. She suggests that what was once a common 'culture of obligation' with Christianity at its heart has become a 'culture of consumption' with many competing world-views on offer for the individual to choose between.

One significant response to this changing context which is very clearly illustrated in collective worship can be seen in the substantial emphasis in recent years on the concept of spirituality. The term 'spiritual' first became central to schools in the 1944 Education Act, but it has received a substantial boost since the 1988 Education Reform Act [section 1.(2)(a)] made the 'spiritual development' of children a clear responsibility of the school. This has been reinforced by the Ofsted requirement to inspect this aspect of school life – in Ofsted reports the criterion most frequently used to measure spiritual development was the perceived adequacy of the acts of collective worship. Webster (1995, p. 90) commented that 'spiritual is a multi-textured word with a long history and many layers of meaning . . .' This quality has led some teachers and educationalists to place it at the centre of their understanding of collective worship. It has the attractive features of being seen as a universal aspect of human experience, which is essentially subjective and personal, and having many forms – both religious and non-religious.

In my interviews one infant school infant teacher spoke of developing 'a little bit of spirituality within the child'; and a junior school teacher described assemblies as 'thinking about spiritual abstractions'. This concept had the advantage that it could be interpreted in both a religious and a non-religious way. As one junior school teacher put it:

> I think worship is only possible if you have in your own mind that there is something there to be worshipped. If you haven't got that concept then worship as such is meaning-less. Spirituality is that other dimension within us all and I believe you can develop that even in people who might not formally say, 'I believe that there is a God' . . . I think even people who do not believe that or whose concept of God is very under-developed will also be, if you could bring it out, . . . aware of something inside us which you and I would call spiritual.

For this teacher, who had a developed idea of spirituality, the term involved, as well as the inward and universal character des-cribed above, 'a sense of awe and wonder, a sense of what a wonderful world we're in, a sense that there is more to life than life, a sense of the transcendental, this sort of thing'. Another junior school teacher described her understanding of the spiritual by saying, 'I try . . . to get across the idea that there is a world beyond the material where there are essential and eternal verities in the light of which we are very small fry.' For some teachers the idea of the spiritual was interpreted in a religious sense. For example: 'the children realize that there is a spiritual side . . . that there is something inside them that is separate that needs to be addressed . . . I think that the bit God deals with is the spiritual' (a junior school teacher).

The idea of spirituality seemed to appeal to some secondary school teachers as a more acceptable framework for assembly. One such teacher commented, 'we do all have a sense of spir-ituality'. The elements he included in his understanding of this concept were: 'some kind of moral touchstone' that 'is external' to ourselves; 'that we have a responsibility to protect the world for generations to come but that is external to me, it is self-less and it is not self-centred'; 'something which is guiding me to think about the way in which I live my life'; and a sense of 'awe and wonder'. This is very close to what a theist might call God, only put in different language. Another secondary school teacher spoke of her understanding of the idea of the spiritual which contained many similar themes:

> Dealing with things that are not material, in the sense of spiritual, things of the spirit, enlarging their understanding that there are more things in the world to care about than just being alive and working. It's about the emotions and feelings and values, and recognizing that there is something else to life than just living . . . [The] feeling of humanity, being human, having needs and recognizing the needs of others, that there is unity among human beings; that there is an appreciation of things like beauty, art and music and those things; things that are dealing with feelings of the spirit rather than a very materialistic world that young people in particular feel is the most important thing.

The school policies also invariably included the notion of spiritual development. However, this was not dealt with in any depth – there were no attempts other than cursory ones to explain what the term might mean. It was usually combined with moral, social and cultural development, and where this happened the emphasis was mostly on common and personal values and the development of personal beliefs. All the infant and junior policies wanted to contribute to the personal development of the children – spiritual, moral, social and cultural (SMSC). Frequently the concept of spiritual development was seen as something which transcended all beliefs. One junior school's SMSC policy stated:

> Spiritual development . . . transcends the potential barriers of religious and cultural difference . . . spiritual growth is not dependent on a child having a secure faith background . . . Spiritual development relates to that aspect of inner life through which pupils acquire insights into their personal existence which are of enduring worth. It is characterised

by reflection, the attribution of meaning to experience, valuing a non-material dimension to life, and intimations of an enduring reality. 'Spiritual' is not synonymous with 'religious'.

This school's collective worship policy spoke of its aim 'to make periods of collective worship "special times", with a distinctly spiritual atmosphere'. Part of this aim was to 'feed the spirit'. The above quotation includes the definition of 'spiritual' offered by Ofsted (1994b) in a discussion paper as 'that aspect of inner life through which pupils acquire insights into their personal existence which are of enduring worth'. This was used by several schools.

The notion of spiritual development was used in all the county secondary schools as a common factor for all pupils, regardless of beliefs. One such school defined 'spiritual' as 'inner self'. Another said, 'the potential for spiritual development is open to everyone and is not confined to the development of religious beliefs'. It is worth noting at this point that the Catholic school made very little use of the term 'spiritual' in its documents. This was largely because it had a very well developed and specific Catholic understanding which did not need to use such a vague and universal term. This does, however, raise the question of whether the notion of a tradition-less spirituality is a valid one, and if so, how it is to be understood.

The notion of spirituality was also present in the government and local authority documents. Some official documents use the idea of the 'spiritual' as an umbrella term to cover moral, religious and other world-views. The School Curriculum and Assessment Authority (SCAA) Discussion Paper No. 3 says:

> The Education Reform Act refers to a dimension of human existence which is termed the 'spiritual' and which applies to all pupils. The potential for spiritual development is open to everyone and is not confined to the development of religious beliefs or conversion to a particular faith.
>
> (SCAA 1995a, p. 3)

Although there has been a considerable amount of discussion of this concept in the official documents (e.g. SCAA Discussion Papers nos. 3 and 6) it remains rather vague and elusive. It is certainly defined in a sense which is primarily individualistic – e.g. 'The essential factor in cultivating spirituality is reflection and learning from one's experience' (SCAA 1996a, p. 7). It is an area which schools find more difficult to handle than moral development. The national picture is that 'pupils' spiritual development remains problematic for most schools' (HMCI report on Standards and Quality in Education 1995–6).

The key features of the concept of 'spirituality' are that it is seen as personal, inward and subjective and yet is a universal feature of human experience. There has been a growing body of opinion among educationalists which has seen this as the way to provide a sound basis for collective worship. Hull (1995) suggested that:

> The set of complex problems facing us will yield to a simple solution: repeal of Section 7 of the Education Reform Act 1988 . . . The expression 'collective worship' should be removed and replaced by 'collective spirituality'. The amended law would require pupils to take part in acts of collective spirituality whose main purpose would be to make a contribution to the spiritual development of the pupils and the school. Problems, controversies and misunderstandings associated with collective worship would disappear, and schools would be provided with a powerful vehicle for promoting spirituality.   (Hull 1995, p. 35)

Priestley (1996) noted the resurgence of interest in the 'spiritual' aspect of education. He argued that this is a reaction to a narrow rationalist and functionalist view of education. The concept of 'spirituality' offers the possibility of a broader vision. He gave some general descriptions of what such a concept might entail (broader than religious, dynamic, to do with being and becoming, other worldly, communal, holistic), but warned against defining it too tightly. There are several other recent publications on spirituality suggesting that many see this as a basis for schools and beyond for dealing with the vexed question of plural beliefs in general and collective worship in particular (e.g. Copley 2000; Wright 2000; Thatcher 1999; Hay with Nye 1998; Hughes and Collins 1996, chapter 5; Brown and Furlong 1996; Webster 1995, chapter 5). Part of its attraction is its emphasis on process (spiritual development) rather than end product (particular moral views or faith commitments) as Erricker (1998, p. 51) has pointed out. Grimmitt (1994) has argued that religious communities need to share in 'a wider common identity'. He suggests that we need to generate a 'spiritual consciousness' and a framework of 'universal spiritual values' (p. 142). However, there are many problems with the concept of spirituality as a sound basis for collective worship in the twenty-first century, and not least its vagueness. The educationalist Terence Copley has also argued that it is a secular, liberal western construct which implies a least common denominator approach (Copley 2000). In the end it seems that, at least in its modern educational form, the concept of spirituality lies within a liberal framework and it is seriously inadequate as a basis for collective worship in county schools in the twenty-first century.

Conclusion

What cannot be avoided, however, is the radical shift since the 1944 Education Act from a context in which one particular religious faith, Christianity, was central to most school communities to a situation in which there is a multiplicity of religious and other world-views and the dominant metaphor is that of the market in which individual consumer choice is paramount. The central conclusion of my research was that this latter view has effectively prevailed in the practice of collective worship and consequently religious belief is essentially treated as 'an individually chosen, private, practical guide to living' – with all the theological and philosophical assumptions which go with such a view. For many people, however, such a situation is far from satisfactory.

CHAPTER 7

Whither Collective Worship?

Introduction

The central argument of this book has been that collective worship is the tip of an iceberg. Beneath the practice of school assemblies lies a plethora of profound issues which also face wider society. A widely acceptable way forward for collective worship will not be found until there has been a deep and widespread analysis of the educational, theological, philosophical, political, sociological and ethical issues which underlie the practice. The current situation in Britain is a result of historical development, largely from the substantial role of the Church in education and the place of Christianity in mainstream culture. The huge changes in British society since the Second World War, described in Chapter 2, have made the current situation anomalous and untenable. Neither the political compromise of the 1988 Education Reform Act between the multicultural and the Christian heritage lobbies, nor the ingenious adaptation of collective worship in the direction of 'worth-ship' and moral and spiritual development by the teaching profession, are satisfactory solutions to the issues. In many ways the practice of collective worship reflects the approach to and understanding of the role of religious belief and spirituality in Britain today. Given that the latter is a very confused picture it is hardly surprising that collective worship is struggling to find a rationale which satisfies all the interested parties.

I will argue in this chapter that the evidence suggests that the current practice of collective worship lies largely within a liberal, rationalist framework which is no longer appropriate for the more genuinely plural context of contemporary Britain. I will then outline some of the features that a rationale for collective worship will need for the future. This will be followed by a description of some of the possible ways forward from the current unsatisfactory quagmire.

The current prevailing approach

I have argued that there is much evidence to show that the actual current practice of collective worship implies a view of religious belief which sees it as an individually chosen, private practical guide to living. This is not necessarily the deliberate intention of those who lead collective worship, but it is implicit in the way it is actually done.

This approach to religious belief reflects primarily a liberal, rationalist framework. This approach begins with the fact that there are many alternative and contradictory world-views. Reasonable people adopt different viewpoints, and it would seem that there is no rational way of deciding between them. If there were then there would be far more agreement than there is. Given this situation the role of the State is to be neutral with regard to competing views of what philosophers call the 'good life'. Its role is the more minimal one of providing a basic framework of justice within which people can live peaceably and follow their own convictions in so far as they do not conflict with the rights of others to follow their (different) views.

Despite the privileged place of Christianity in the 1988 Education Reform Act, most of the teachers did not want to be seen to be favouring Christianity in the sense of implying it is superior to other faiths and world-views. What was central was the emphasis on each individual's freedom of choice, the need for mutual respect and understanding of diverse views, and the stress on a common moral framework which allowed this diversity to live together in a harmonious manner – i.e. core liberal values. A multiplicity of 'private' views of the good life was not only tolerated, it was seen as something to be celebrated and affirmed as adding richness and colour to life and as increasing the choices open to each individual to fashion their lives as they will. However, there are many problems with this liberal framework and it is seriously inadequate as a basis for collective worship in county schools.

The crumbling liberal paradigm

There are many critiques of liberalism. They come from a variety of perspectives, most of which have their own (different) philosophy of education. I have already described some critiques: Muslim (Halstead and Khan-Cheema 1987; Muslim Educational Forum 1997), Christian (Newbigin 1989; Thiessen 1993; Wright 1993; Cooling 1994), postmodern (Usher and Edwards 1994), conservative (Tate 1996); and philosophical (Polanyi 1958; MacIntyre 1988; Gill 1992; Sacks 1991 and 1995). There is enough in these arguments to make us realize that liberalism is struggling to retain its hegemonic position in an increasingly plural and postmodern world. Although it still has a crucial role as a bulwark against fundamentalism and intolerance, it can lead to a relativistic understanding of religious belief and other world-views which is unacceptable to many. More and more people are arguing that it is properly seen as one world-view among many and, as such, its view of religious belief should be treated accordingly – it is not the only show in town. McLaughlin (1992, p. 240) has suggested that liberalism rests on a core of non-contested public values: it is becoming increasingly difficult to identify what these might be as society becomes more plural in character.

Many of the key issues in the current collective worship debate depend crucially on the liberal framework for their validity. These issues are often seen very differently from within other world-views. There are at least four such issues.

The first of these is the distinction between knowledge and belief. The beginning of modern philosophy is often traced back to the seventeenth-century philosopher Descartes with his emphasis on the individual thinking person and his quest for certain knowledge. The shift that took place in the West from the mediaeval period to the Enlightenment was from a reliance on the Bible and Christian tradition as the primary foundation of true knowledge to a reliance on our sensory experience and logical rational thinking. There arose a powerful belief that there was one form of rationality with which every human being, if they were thinking aright, would agree. The impact of the rise of science in the seventeenth century was colossal and strongly reinforced this trend. Very crudely speaking this trend reached its philosophical zenith in the Logical Positivist school of thought, as exemplified by

Ayer (1936) who consigned all moral, aesthetic and religious language to the realm of subjective opinion. The paradigms for knowledge were mathematics with its reliance on logic, and science with its reliance on sensory experience and rational thought. The meaning and reliability of the interpretation of sense data has been much discussed by philosophers and there are different schools of thought on how this is to be seen (e.g. realists and idealists), but there can be little doubt that in the modern Western world the paradigm of knowledge has been very substantially influenced by science and empiricism. We have already discussed Hirst's understanding of the nature of knowledge and its impact on religious education in the 1960s and beyond.

There are many, from a variety of different perspectives, who have disputed this sharp division. Both the philosopher Alasdair MacIntyre and the theologian Lesslie Newbigin dispute the clear division between 'facts' and 'opinions'. The scientist Michael Polanyi (1958), in an inquiry into the nature and justification of scientific knowledge, coined the phrase 'personal knowledge' to describe his approach. He started 'by rejecting the ideal of scientific detachment' which 'falsifies our whole outlook far beyond the domain of science'. He argued against the idea that true knowledge is 'impersonal, universally established, objective' – rather, he suggested 'all acts of understanding' involve the '*personal participation* of the knower'. This does not lead to an arbitrary subjectivity; he says:

> Comprehension is neither an arbitrary act nor a passive experience, but a responsible act claiming universal validity. Such knowing is indeed *objective* in the sense of establishing contact with a hidden reality . . . It seems reasonable to describe this fusion of the personal and the objective as Personal Knowledge. (pp. vii-viii)

Writing from a Roman Catholic perspective, Arthur (1995, p. 47) also disputes the clear division between knowledge and belief. He comments:

> Faith and human knowledge need to be integrated so that religious truth informs the whole of life and understanding. Education is not simply the application of secular knowl-

edge to a secular world; on the contrary, the Church insists that truth and human knowledge are in profound harmony, so that all knowledge and understanding is touched and transformed by the truths about human beings and God which are taught by faith. The embodiment of this vision is the purpose of Catholic education.

The division between knowledge and belief is subsumed under a broader total view of life, as is the understanding of education. A similar attitude can be found in other religious viewpoints. We do not need to consider all the arguments about this division between knowledge and belief, but merely note that in world-views other than the liberal, rationalist one this division is often not so clear.

The second issue which depends on the liberal, rationalist framework is the public/private distinction. Religious education-alist Andrew Wright (1998) traces important strands of the liberal position back to Locke, who stressed the fact that what we can know with certainty (from our sense experiences) is relatively little: we depend for most of our living and behaviour on contingent beliefs and opinions (and, for Locke, religious beliefs fall into this category). The question then arises as to how people of diverse views are to live together harmoniously given that there is no rational way of knowing for certain which views are correct. Wright suggests that 'Locke's liberalism flows equally from his philosophical theory and political practice.' Mid-seventeenth-century England was confronted with many deep and conflicting religious views. Locke's solution was to develop the distinction between private religious belief and public policy. This view was born out of conflict primarily as an ethical view on how competing convictions might live together peacefully, but it was also, importantly, dependent upon Locke's theory of know-ledge which drew a clear line between knowledge and belief.

However, there are at least two main problems with this distinction today. The first is that many religious people simply do not accept that their religious belief is confined to their private lives. For them it is a total viewpoint which affects all areas of life. This suggests that the public/private division depends on the liberal framework. The second problem is that what began life as an ethical view has hardened into an epistemological theory.

Mutual respect and tolerance for different religious views does not necessarily mean that they need all be regarded as equally valid interpretations of experience and there is no way of choosing rationally between them. Wright (1998) argues that liberal religious education has been built on liberalism as a 'comprehensive world-view committed to its own distinctive beliefs and morality' and this has tended to suppress consideration of conflicting truth-claims which are central to religious traditions, and so produces religiously illiterate pupils who do not understand the nature of these faiths. What is needed to avoid this 'imperialistic liberal discourse', he suggests, is that we should recognize the 'existence of a plurality of perspectives', and encourage 'open debate between alternative liberal and non-liberal traditions'. This means shifting from a 'hard' understanding of liberalism as a total world-view to a 'soft notion of liberalism as an interim political ethic', which is much more in line with Locke's original intention. He sees the 'true battle ahead' as 'between soft and hard forms of liberalism: between a liberalism that has come of age and a liberalism still struggling with its adolescent identity'. Again, the key point to note is that the private/public distinction depends on the liberal framework, and for a plural world some adaptation of this framework will be needed.

The third issue in the collective worship debate which depends on the liberal rationalist framework is the sharp distinction between education and nurture. Most of the teachers in my sample had a very strong fear of indoctrination. They saw themselves as educators in the sense that their aim was to produce independent, rational, freethinking people who would make their own well-informed choices in such disputed areas as religion and some areas of morality. They should be free as individuals to fashion their lives according to their own choices. Freedom of choice was the highest good in this schema, not any sense of choosing the 'right' or the 'true'. In other words, there was no common sense of what the 'good life' might mean: it was taken for granted that a multiplicity of views existed. Now as a matter of empirical fact this is undoubtedly true. However, this freedom of choice which begins as an ethical view can, and very often did in my sample, become an effective epistemology which suggests that there really are no rational grounds for choosing one view rather than another. But this is an example of the 'hard liberalism' of which Wright (1998) spoke. When seen from other viewpoints you certainly can evaluate different conceptions of the good life, albeit on grounds that are internal to that world-view. Most devout Muslims, for example, are in little doubt that their beliefs are right. As mentioned in Chapter 4, traditional understandings of education see the primary function of education as being to pass on received wisdom and knowledge to the next generation. If you hold that a view gives real insight into the truth of the matter in some absolute sense, then the purpose of education is to help the pupil to gain that insight and to nurture them in a correct understanding of life. In a traditional philosophy of education this is as important as teaching the correctness of the theory of gravity. Thiessen (1993) has given a detailed defence of religious nurture against the charge of indoctrination, partly by giving a critique of the prevailing view of liberal education. He suggests that we need a new ideal of liberal education based on a more open recognition of basic under-lying beliefs. This would lead to a greater diversity of schooling given the plurality of belief-systems, of which liberalism, or at least a 'hard' form of liberalism, is only one.

The fourth issue dependent on the liberal framework is the great emphasis on the individual as the primary unit at the expense of any conception of community. However, many are now pointing to the importance of the community in moral and personal education (e.g. MacIntyre 1988; Gill 1992; Sacks 1991 and 1995). The idea of a free-floating, neutral individual who is given basic information and then takes a 'free' decision about basic beliefs and commitments is a myth. People are formed in com-munities – families, faiths, and others – which have their own traditions in which the individual is nurtured. Of course, at a later stage any given person can decide to reject the traditions of his or her nurturing community, but everyone is part of some such community – and liberal education itself is one such tradition of beliefs.

The end of the liberal paradigm?

The roots of liberalism were in a context of seventeenth-century conflict between competing religious views – and in the fear of the fragmentation and wars which ensued. It has been enormously successful in providing a framework for diversity. However, it has increased its scope from a primarily ethical stance to an all-embracing world-view which has difficulty accepting the challenges of non-liberal traditions to its very fabric. Liberalism has provided the basis for public education and it is strongly reflected in, for example, the Swann Report of 1985. My data has shown that it is still the dominant influence on teachers in their approach to religious belief in the context of collective worship. In many respects they reflect the multicultural approach of the Swann Report which stressed the equal validity of different world-views.

For the reasons given above it looks increasingly unlikely that the liberal framework, certainly in its 'hard' format, will be adequate for today's plural and postmodern world. Several writers have suggested that we are at a point of transition when a new paradigm will be needed, akin to Kuhn's notion of a paradigm shift in science when a whole new conceptual system is needed to account for a radically different situation (Kuhn 1962). Sacks (1991, p. 20), writing from a Jewish perspective, claimed:

> We are nearing the end of a period in human civilisation in which there seemed to be no limits to individual choice and collective reason. Traditions had been deconstructed and technical reason took their place. Ends were things individually chosen, and the machinery of science and government provided the means. Within this promethean vision, religion could lead at most a diminishing and marginal existence.
>
> But already this social and intellectual world has lost its plausibility. Enlightenment ended in Holocaust . . .
>
> We are caught between two ages, one passing, the other not yet born, and the conflicting tendencies we witness – deepening secularisation on the one hand, new religious passions on the other – are evidence of the transition.

Sacks is in no doubt that the liberal vision of pluralism in which 'society is a neutral arena of private choices where every vision of the good carries its own credentials of authority' (p. 88) is not only no longer adequate in today's world, but also deeply damaging to the fabric of society.

Usher and Edwards (1994) are concerned with insights from postmodernism, despite the difficulty they admit of accurately characterizing the term. They say:

> We take the view that education is itself going through profound change in terms of purposes, content and methods. These changes are part of a process that, generally, questions the role of education as the child of the Enlightenment. Consequently, education is currently the site of conflict and part of the stakes in that conflict.   (p. 3)

Part of the reason for this change is that:

> Education does not fit easily into the postmodern moment because educational theory and practice is founded in the modernist tradition. Education is very much the dutiful child of the Enlightenment and, as such, tends to uncritically accept a set of assumptions deriving from Enlightenment thought. Indeed it is possible to see education as the vehicle by which the Enlightenment ideals of critical reason, humanistic individual freedom and benevolent progress are substantiated and realised.   (p. 24)

Amongst other things, postmodernism challenges the concepts of the self, rationality, and objective knowledge – all of which are central to liberal education.

The main point to note from all these writers is the suggestion that the classic liberal paradigm of education will no longer meet the needs of a genuinely plural and postmodern education. The evidence from my data suggests that teachers are still working within this liberal paradigm as far as collective worship goes, but it involves them personally in very considerable tensions, as already described. I take this to be supportive evidence for the contention that a new framework of understanding is needed if the collective worship debate is to move on. It is insoluble on the basis of liberalism, and recent efforts to find a way forward have inevitably floundered (e.g. R.E. Council 1998).

The way forward – a new plural, critical realist paradigm

In this final section I shall, on the basis of my data and its analysis, suggest some of the characteristics which will be needed by a new paradigm for education that will be adequate to cope with the issues raised by the current practice of collective worship in schools.

A genuinely plural paradigm

A new paradigm needs to live openly and honestly with deep differences of view. Some world-views profoundly disagree with the consigning of fundamental beliefs to a notional 'private', individual sphere, as the Muslim and Catholic understandings of education show very clearly. This would entail a proper recognition that there are different 'rationalities' rather than one overarching objective, context-free 'Rationality' as posited by Enlightenment liberalism (see MacIntyre 1988; Usher and Edwards 1994, p. 27). This means that different traditions and rationalities will each have to develop their own understanding of pluralism as, for example, Hick (1989) and many others have attempted from within the Christian tradition. This is no optional extra, but a central and urgent task facing any tradition which sees itself as offering an understanding of human life. It must be able to give a coherent account of how it relates to other, possibly competing, traditions.

Part of this understanding of pluralism must be a sophisticated account of the relationship between the absolute claims of a tradition and the relativizing tendency of a plural context. What is the nature of absolute commitments in a plural situation? How do we avoid a hard, exclusive fundamentalism on the one hand, and an easy-going, all-embracing relativism on the other? Sacks (1991, 105–6) points to the need for a plural theology which avoids both liberalism and fundamentalism and is such that 'religions can be both faithful to their traditions and answerable to the imperative of tolerance'. Hart (1995, pp. 90ff.) seeks to find a basis for Christian theology which finds a way between an over-confident objectivism and an agnostic relativism. O'Leary (1996) brings ideas from both the Buddhist and Christian traditions together with insights from postmodern philosophers to consider the questions, 'How true are the great religions?' and 'How are they true?' He argues that theology must be 'phenomenological' – rooted in experience, 'pluralistic' – open to diversity, and 'rational' – based on reason. He comments:

> All three approaches are concerned with truth. The first is concerned with the 'truth of revelation' . . . The second attempts to show that within the always limited and contingent horizons of a pluralistic religious universe it is possible for a discourse to refer objectively to an absolute truth or truths, though this truth can never be . . . formulated independently of the interplay between divergent discourses. The third will focus more sharply on the ultimate rational justification for maintaining religious claims . . .
>
> (O'Leary 1996, p. xii)

O'Leary provides a sophisticated attempt to grapple with these issues, and there are many others undertaking a similar task. The point to be made here is not to evaluate these attempts, but to emphasize the fact that they are taking the plural context seriously. Such thinking is essential for providing a satisfactory basis for collective worship in schools.

A paradigm which emphasizes the importance of communities, traditions of faith and fiduciary frameworks

I have already cited the work of MacIntyre (1988), Gill (1992) and Sacks (1991), all of whom stress the importance of traditions and continuing communities in the shaping of a person's world-view. This is in contrast with the liberal myth of isolated, free, autonomous individuals who are being given the wherewithal to make their choices and so shape their lives 'from scratch' beginning with a 'blank sheet'. We are all formed in some community or another which will have its own particular traditions, norms, values and beliefs. Mitchell (1994, pp. 357ff.) expresses the balance needed between the nurturing community and the individual when he asks, 'Can the individual learn to be either critical or creative without first having been inducted into a continuing tradition of some kind?' He then quotes Gilbert Murray to summarize his view:

Every man who possesses real vitality can be seen as the resultant of two forces. He is first the child of a particular age, society, convention; of what we may call in one word a tradition. He is, secondly, in one degree or another, a rebel against that tradition. And the best traditions make the best rebels. (quoted by Mitchell 1994, p. 358)

Two notes of caution need to be added here. First, are we to assume that traditions have an integrity to them and do not have fuzzy edges or porous boundaries? In today's postmodern world it is often suggested that a profound eclecticism is at work which allows people to borrow from different traditions to build their own. Second, it is not obvious of which traditions or communities any given person is a part. Might not the typical school pupil be a member of several communities, each with its own language and rationality?

Just as MacIntyre has drawn attention to the socially embodied character of traditions of rationality and so undermined the liberal concept of the autonomous rational individual, so Polanyi (1958) has pointed out the need for a 'fiduciary framework' within which to operate. Complete scepticism is not possible; we have to take some things for granted if we are to know anything. The ideal of detached, certain, objective knowledge is a chimera. Polanyi (1958, p. 265) says:

When the supernatural authority of laws, churches and sacred texts had waned or collapsed, man tried to avoid the emptiness of mere self-assertion by establishing over himself the authority of experience and reason. But it has now turned out that modern scientism fetters thought as cruelly as ever the churches had done. It offers no scope for our most vital beliefs and it forces us to disguise them in farcically inadequate terms.

Polanyi suggests that Locke's sharp distinction between empirically and rationally demonstrable knowledge and subjective faith which had no such certainty was deeply unsatisfactory:

We must now recognize belief once more as the source of all knowledge. Tacit assent and intellectual passions, the sharing of an idiom and of a cultural heritage, affiliation to a like-minded community: such are the impulses which shape our vision of the nature of things on which we rely for our mastery of things. No intelligence, no matter how critical or original, can operate outside such a fiduciary framework. (Polanyi 1958, p. 266)

He turns back to Augustine's maxim *'nisi credideritis, non intelligitis'* (unless it is believed, it cannot be understood) to provide a more satisfactory basis for knowledge than Cartesian scepticism and Enlightenment rationalism. We all need some basic beliefs or 'fiduciary framework' within which to operate, and this needs to be made explicit. As Hart (1995, p. 69) expresses it:

At the end of the day both objectivism and relativism founder on the same erroneous assumption; namely that it is possible to transcend one's particularity in an absolute manner, gaining access to a view of reality which is no-one's in particular, the view from nowhere.

There is no such thing as the 'view from nowhere'. We all make basic assumptions in the way we live – and this includes those who adopt a hard form of liberalism. The crucial thing is to recognize what is going on and to make any 'fiduciary framework' explicit.

The need for conversation and dialogue

Once we admit that people can belong to fundamentally different traditions of rationality or adopt varying 'fiduciary frameworks' we are opening the door to fragmentation and the inability to communicate with one another. The Enlightenment belief in an overarching, universal, neutral, context-free rationality offered the tempting possibility of a language which all could learn and an authority which all would accept. However, as we have seen, this was to prove a false god. A new way of communication has to be found in a genuinely plural world in order to promote real respect, tolerance and understanding. The teachers in my sample were well aware of the crucial importance of this communication and worked hard to achieve a united school which recognized and celebrated its diverse components. There was a deep fear of fragmentation which led at times to a superficial approach to differences which tended to relativize them and avoid deep areas of conflict. In some respects this reduced the possibility of genuine understanding and communication between faith-traditions because it focused mainly on the similarities, or sought to place all traditions within a liberal, rational framework.

At a practical level, the Christian Education Movement has produced a guide to interfaith relations in schools which makes some important points. First, 'Each faith tradition sees itself as worthy of consideration in its own right rather than in terms of another' (CEM 1996, p. 4). Second, it recognizes that there are disagreements over sources of authority and, therefore, 'What we have to aim for is a respectful disagreement . . . Telling each other's story . . . and listening to it' (pp. 34–5). It suggests that 'If the greater mingling of people of different faiths has brought their differences into sharper focus, it has also presented unparalleled opportunities for dialogue and real understanding' (p. 38).

But more is needed than good intentions to listen respectfully. We need a proper understanding of how communication takes place between different groups and its underlying theory and purpose. Of course, each tradition will have to produce its own views on this matter. I have already mentioned the ideas of MacIntyre (1988) and Sacks (1991 and 1995), both of whom use the analogy of speaking different languages: MacIntyre of learning a 'second first language' and Sacks of speaking a 'first language' of common citizenship and a 'second language' of communal identity. Nipkow (1993) has also provided some useful insights. He distinguishes between a 'soft' pluralism which tends to look for universal solutions or a 'pluralistic supersystem' (common spiritual experience, similar religious praxis, overlapping elements, religions as many ways to the one God) and a 'hard' pluralism which stresses the incommensurability of different systems and their individual claims to ultimacy. He suggests that the former can end up as a dogmatic relativism which prescribes an ecumenical 'Esperanto' that 'will neither acknowledge the full, rich, authentic individual (religious) languages nor solve the problems of a 'hard' (religious) pluralism' (p. 8). The latter presents the real danger of fragmentation and intolerance. His research among young people in Germany suggests that these issues are no longer central to them because they 'no longer share such authentic religious experiences in specific religious communities' (p. 8). They displayed an '*a priori* relativism' which saw all religions as 'mere variations of the one' (p. 9) – the only thing that really mattered was the reality and meaning of 'God'. They also tended to 'look at everything in the field of religion from a *functional* and a highly *individualised* perspective' (p. 8). The former of these meant that they focused on the psychological and moral usefulness of religious beliefs, and the latter implied a 'poignant *subjectivity*: "God is for everyone what he or she believes God to be"' (p. 8). This corresponds closely with the findings of my research, which has suggested that religious belief is treated in a relative, subjective, individual and functional manner in the context of collective worship. The issue of conflicting truth-claims is taking second place to the efficacy of faith. This has the effect of taking attention away from the need to translate and communicate between faiths and rationalities and focusing instead on the need for understanding of what it means to follow a particular faith. This trend can reduce the possibilities of genuine dialogue.

A concern for 'truth'

Does this mean that we should simply give up on the idea of 'realist' understandings of life which suggest that there is something 'beyond' our ideas and concepts to which we are trying, more or less successfully, to respond? Is the concept of 'truth' merely internal to a particular conceptual system, and the only thing that matters is whether or not it provides the individual with what they consider to be an satisfactory world-view? There are many who would argue that such an approach is profoundly unsatisfactory. Cardinal Hume (1998, p. 5) said:

> There is . . . an attitude towards the truths of religion which can be very undermining. It is called relativism. Relativism does not simply say that the claims of religion are false. Instead, it attempts to short-circuit any discussion about truth. The relativist says 'There is no truth, there are only opinions. You do your thing; and I'll do mine'. In the guise of tolerance it promotes indifference; in the guise of intellectual honesty, a radical irrationality. For there is no basis for argument and dialogue, or of explanation. Rival values, moral teachings, ideals and religions about what makes for human fulfilment and happiness are simply labelled like

products on a shelf. You take your pick. Which way of life or religion you prefer becomes yet another consumer choice.

Hume, building on the papal encyclical *Veritatis Splendor*, calls for 'a rediscovery of revelation – the ultimate truth which is disclosed to us of our origin and ultimate destiny'.

There have been several calls for a greater prominence to be given in education to the concept of truth. Baelz (1995, p. 28) considers the tradition of university education and raises the problem of the view that all criteria of rationality and truth are culturally embedded. He concludes by saying, 'Dare we suggest that our university today should strive to be a community that transmits from generation to generation what we may call "the question of Truth"?' Orchard (1992, p. 3), coming from a Christian viewpoint, suggests that 'the overall goal of education is immense, nothing less than the pursuit of ultimate truth'. Watson (1987, p. 15) argues that education must involve the search for truth. Wright (1993, chapter 4) suggests that current RE tends to ignore the crucial question of the truth claims of religions and this is, in his view, highly unsatisfactory.

A concern for 'truth', even given all the difficulties involved, is an essential pillar of any satisfactory paradigm for collective worship. If this issue is marginalized, as has happened in the current practice of collective worship in my sample schools, it is very easy to fall into an implicit relativism and the consequence is often indifference to such questions.

The implications for collective worship and education in general

A greater diversity of schooling

The myth of the neutral, common school can no longer be maintained. Schools which firmly embrace a hard, liberal ideology should be seen as one type of school amongst many. The fundamental beliefs and values on which the school is built need to be openly declared and this will lead to a greater diversity of schooling. The movement in this direction can be seen in many places. The government 'white paper' entitled *Choice and Diversity* (DFE 1992, p. 1) affirmed this trend and the important place within the state sector of 'voluntary schools provided by the churches and other voluntary bodies with their distinctive ethos and traditions'. Muslim schools have recently been granted 'aided' status, and the Anglican schools are developing their distinctive identity further in a newly confident manner (Carey, Hope and Hall 1998). There has been in recent years a very deliberate programme of increasing school diversity encouraging schools to differentiate themselves according to ethos and areas of specialist expertise. Usher and Edwards (1994, pp. 210ff.) have suggested that education for the 'postmodern moment' should be

> more diverse in terms of goals and processes and consequently in terms of organisational structures, curricula, methods and participants. Education would 'take its cue' from the diverse cultural contexts in which it was located rather than from universal logocentric norms. Instead of seeking to reduce everything to the 'same' it would become instead the vehicle for the celebration of diversity, a space for different voices against the one authoritative 'voice' of modernity.

The schools in my sample did make a point of trying to celebrate diversity, but this was done within a framework of liberal rationalism rather than a plural framework.

Holmes (1992) sees the two main dangers facing common schools in plural cultures as, on the one hand, 'centrifugalism and disintegration' if there is too much choice, and on the other hand a 'bland common school' which has only a low level of ethos and tradition and thereby appeals to no one. His solution is to maintain a 'strong consensual program for the majority and dissenting schools for the minority' (p. 128) as this will maintain the cohesion and central identity of society. The common schools should have certain basic features required of them, but they should also seek to develop their own distinctive ethos building on their own tradition and local circumstances – so, for example, religion could be a central feature of some common schools, or a particular cultural background.

The present situation with collective worship in schools is significantly compromised. On the one hand the 1988 Education Reform Act and subsequent legislation, combined with Circular 1/94 and the Ofsted inspection procedures, can seem to be a crude attempt to impose a cultural imperialism in a vain attempt to re-establish a past, apparently more homogeneous Christian society; on the other hand the legislative framework recognizes the plurality of cultures and tries not to make evaluative comments about the validity of different faiths. The outworking of this in my sample schools is largely undertaken within a liberal, rationalist framework of education which itself imposes certain understandings of religious belief in an imperialistic manner. One possible way forward is to accept a greater variety of schooling within the state system which would allow those schools which wished to adopt a secular, humanist ethos to do so openly; and similarly those which wanted to adopt a more religious ethos would be free to do so.

Education for a plural world

Wright (1998) points to the danger of producing 'religiously illiterate' pupils if we avoid dealing with issues of competing truth-claims in RE. In my sample schools this avoidance was occurring on a large scale in collective worship. The danger with this approach to collective worship is that it leads almost inevitably to an unsatisfactory view of religious belief with the attendant dangers of indifference, a facile relativism which implies that religious choices do not matter, or an isolated individualism which idolizes individual freedom and neglects the importance of community and tradition. Children need more than this if they are to be equipped to live in a plural world. Bolton (1997, p. 135) argues that a phenomenological approach to religions is not sufficient. We must also ask, 'Are all world-views equally valid?' and 'give to children the tools of evaluation'. He is not very clear about what those tools might be, but the point I support is the need to make evaluations about beliefs. A similar comment is made by Astley (1994, p. 287) when he considers the position of the Christian learner:

> For all educators the problem of *relativity* is an important issue. Whatever the content being taught, the Christian learner faces the challenge of an actually or potentially vast variety of viewpoints – a variety of 'truths'. Even if she comes to believe that there is one set of absolute truths underlying this variety, she must still learn how to cope with this variety herself, how to relate to other people of

different persuasions, and how to educate others to live in a world of relativity.

The present arrangements for collective worship do not help children to live in a 'world of relativity' (I prefer the term 'world of plurality') because too many substantial points of conflict are avoided and the whole activity takes place under the umbrella of liberal rationalism which leads inexorably to a highly unsatisfactory understanding of religious belief. Under a veneer of neutrality children are being inducted into a tradition – that of liberalism and its view of religious belief. A new paradigm is needed along the lines described above if the issue of collective worship in schools is to find a way out of its present confusion.

Options for the future

The first defensible position is that of the status quo. There is a strong argument, as put forward for example by the Church of England Board of Education, that daily collective worship is the right of every child and should be maintained as part of the pupils' educational experience. There is sufficient scope and flexibility within the existing legislation to accommodate denominations and faiths other than the Church of England, especially in the provision for withdrawal and determinations. Thousands of schools have a record of good practice in daily collective worship. Many schools have found ways of implementing the legislation in a manner which respects the integrity of those involved. A further, negative argument for the status quo is the lack of agreement on any alternative – so stick with what we have. This view has political inertia in its favour. Every time that legislation is debated in this area it proves deeply contentious and the practicalities of demands upon government time mean that it is only worth beginning the process of legislative change if there is a reasonable amount of prior agreement about where the debate might end. The obvious problem with this view is that it fails to address the current unease – and this unease has been around for many years and shows no signs of going away. Preserving the status quo may be a necessary short-term political compromise. It cannot be satisfactory in the longer term.

A second option would be to proscribe collective worship in any overt and traditional religious sense – i.e. move closer towards the position of the USA and France which maintains a separation between state schools and the religious faith. Leave all the nurturing of belief to families and to the faith communities on the grounds that religion is essentially a private matter and the State should not play any part in promoting any particular faith. Undoubtedly some teachers and many others would welcome such a move. Assemblies could still be opportunities for moral or general spiritual reflection on the nature of life and how it should be lived, as advocated, for example, by the British Humanist Association and the National Secular Society. This approach fails to account for the continuing popularity of religious assemblies among parents and support from many faith communities. It also introduces an artificial distinction which by disallowing talk of pupils' faiths – a real part of their sense of identity and purpose – could reduce assembly to an anodyne least-common-denominator affair that failed to connect with the deep formative beliefs of many of the participants. There is the further argument that given the history of this country proscription would effectively be a loss of heritage.

Third, some – notably Professor John Hull – have argued for acts of collective spirituality. The advantage of that approach is that it would be a move to give a more universal appeal to the whole process given that spirituality is seen as an aspect of all human life. It might also mean that the non-material considerations of basic questions of human value are given an assured place. There has been a considerable literature on the notion of spiritual education as a possible theoretical foundation for collective worship (e.g. Thatcher 1999, Copley 2000, Wright 2000). The main attraction is that spirituality is seen as a universal human trait. Everyone has some spirituality whether in a religious or non-religious form. It is seen as an inner, personal thing, but the problem is that it is such a vague notion that it can degenerate into an almost vacuous one. Precisely because it is so vague the idea of spirituality is in danger of manipulation or drift of content by teachers, either wittingly or unwittingly, and the moral and spiritual formation of children becomes the result of the individual choices of their educators which might be made on any number of grounds. It can further be argued that the concept of spirituality is a product of the liberal paradigm and is a last-ditch attempt to maintain its hegemonic position in education.

Copley (2000, p. 135) concludes that the language of spirituality in education is dominated by secular models. He says, 'spiritual development is a liberal western construct, locked into a secular base of a multi-cultural society in which truth questions are avoided at all costs and the truth is merely what "I" conceive it to be.' A generalized spirituality is fraught with problems and dangers.

Last, there could be a deliberate promotion of a greater diversity of types of school, each with its own distinctive ethos and values and allowing each school to declare its position. There would need to be certain limits if these schools were to be publicly funded. Such a move is already happening with the advent of Muslim schools, and the promotion of specialist schools, within the state system. If there is too much diversity we face the problem of fragmentation and disintegration; if there is too little diversity we face the problem of having bland common schools whose only values are the minimum ones to ensure the school community can live together. Encouraging schools to develop their own distinctive ethos based on their own tradition and local circumstances might be considered as a real option, allowing each school to make its own choice about the content of assemblies. Such a position would be far more honest than the current one. There has been a considerable move in this direction already as a result of several government initiatives. In the famous words of Alastair Campbell we are moving away from the 'bog-standard, one-size-fits-all comprehensive' towards a much greater diversity of schooling in many areas. This diversity could also apply to the underlying ethos of the school, which should be made very clear and open. At present the prevailing liberal ethos tends to be either hidden or assumed. It is not explicitly stated as one ethos amongst other perfectly acceptable ones.

Clearly the danger of such a move is that of fragmentation, as has been forcibly expressed in the continuing debate over the desirability of faith schools. Within such a framework of diversity there would need to be some general requirements about the need to encourage attitudes of respect and understanding between differing world-views – i.e. basic tools for living peaceably and well in a plural culture. This is not simply a retreat to the liberal view that religion is a private matter, but a much more open and honest stating of basic values and encouraging pupils to learn how to live secure in a particular tradition, but knowledgeable about and able to relate well to those of other traditions.

There is unlikely to be any move on the vexed question of collective worship in schools until these deeper questions of how we are to live as a genuinely plural culture are thoroughly explored. We cannot go on trying to shoe-horn everyone into a liberal approach to religious belief which the current practice entails. A new paradigm is needed along the lines described above if the issue of collective worship in schools is to find a way out of its present confusion. The issues beneath the tip of the collective worship iceberg are reflected in wider society and the resolution of them has implications far beyond the world of education. The need to address them is vital. Icebergs are ignored at our collective peril.

Bibliography

Ainsworth, J. and Brown, A. (1995) *Moral Education*. London, The National Society.

Almond, B. (1988) 'Conflict or compromise? Religious and moral education in a plural context' in McLelland, V. Alan (ed.) *Christian Education in a Plural Society*. London, Routledge, pp. 101–16.

Alves, Colin (1968) *Religion and the Secondary School*. London, SCM Press.

Alves, Colin (1989) 'R.E. and Collective Worship in Schools. The Thinking Behind the Act'. *Head Teachers Review* Spring 1989, pp. 12–15.

Alves, Colin (1991) 'Just a matter of words? The Religious Education Debate in the House of Lords'. *British Journal of Religious Education* 13.3, pp. 168–74.

Anderson, Walter Truett (ed.) (1996) *The Fontana Postmodern Reader*. London, Fontana.

Arthur, James (1995) *The Ebbing Tide: Policy and Principles of Catholic Education*. Leominster, Gracewing Fowler Wright.

Ashraf, Syed Ali (1997) 'The Islamic Response: Faith-based education in a multi-faith, multi-cultural country' in Shortt, J. and Cooling, T. (eds) *Agenda for Educational Change*. Leicester, Apollos, pp. 269–79.

Association of Christian Teachers (1990) *School Assembly and the Christian Teacher*. Briefing Paper 4. St Albans, ACT.

Association of Teachers and Lecturers (1995) *Collective Worship: Policy and Practice. Throwing out the baby with the bathwater?* London, ATL.

Astley, J. (1994) *The Philosophy of Christian Religious Education*. London, SPCK.

Ayer, A. J. (1936) *Language, Truth and Logic*. London, Penguin.

Baelz, P. (1995) 'True religion and sound learning'. *Theology*, vol. xcviii, no. 781, Jan/Feb. 1995, pp. 19–28.

Ballard, Paul (1966) 'Discussing Morning Worship'. *Learning for Living* 6.2, pp. 16–19.

Barber, Michael (1998) *The ethics of educational reform*. Address to the SHA conference 21 March 1998.

Barnes, L. Philip (1997) 'Religion, Religionism and Religious Education'. *Journal of Education and Christian Belief*, 1.1, Spring 1997, pp. 7–23.

Barrow, Robin and White, Patricia (eds) (1993) *Beyond Liberal Education: Essays in Honour of Paul H. Hirst*. London, Routledge.

Barton, David et al. (1994) *Open the Door: Guidelines for Worship and for the Inspection of Worship in Voluntary and Grant-maintained Church Schools*. London, Oxford Diocesan Educational Services and the National Society.

BBC Education (1989) *Together: An Assembly for Schools*. London, BBC Enterprises.

Beck, John (1998) *Morality and Citizenship Education*. London, Cassell.

Bedfordshire Education Service (1985) *Religious Education – A Planning Guide*. Ampthill, Bedfordshire Education Service.

Bedfordshire Education Service (1995) *Guidelines for Writing a School Collective Worship Policy*. Bedford, Bedfordshire Education Service.

Bellah, Robert et al. (1985) *Habits of the Heart: Middle America Observed*. Berkeley, University of California Press.

Bellah, R. N. (1976) *Beyond Belief: Essays on Religion in a Post-traditional World*. New York, Harper and Row.

Berger, P. and Kellner, H. (1981) *Sociology Reinterpreted*. Harmondsworth, Penguin.

Berger, P. and Luckmann, K. (1966) *The Social Construction of Reality*. London, Penguin.

Bernstein, B. et al. (1971) 'Ritual in Education' in Cosin, B. R. et al. (eds) *School and Society: a Sociological Reader*. London, Routledge and Kegan Paul/Open University Press.

Birmingham City Council Education Department (1993) *Collective Worship in Birmingham: Policy Guidelines for County Schools and Colleges*. Birmingham City Council Education Department.

Blight, T. (1994) *An Investigation into the Theological and Philosophical Implications of the Requirements for Collective Worship in County Schools from 1944 to 1994, with Special Reference to Three County Schools in the London Borough of Newham*. MA dissertation, King's College, London.

Board of Education of the General Synod of the Church of England (1996) *Tomorrow is Another Country: Education in a Post-modern World*. London, Church House Publishing.

Bolton, Andrew (1997) 'Should Religious Education Foster National Consciousness?' *British Journal of Religious Education*. 19.3, pp. 134–41.

Bowen, J. (1972) *A History of Western Education. Vol. 1. 2000BC – AD1054.* London, Methuen.

Braithwaite, R. B. (1971) 'An Empiricist's View of the Nature of Religious Belief' in Mitchell, B. (ed.) *The Philosophy of Religion.* London, Oxford University Press, pp. 72–91.

Brierley, Peter (1991) *'Christian' England: What the English Church Census Reveals.* London, Marc Europe.

Brimer, James (1972) 'School Worship with Juniors.' *Learning for Living* 11.5, pp. 6–12.

British Council of Churches (1989) *Worship in Education.* London, British Council of Churches.

British Humanist Association (1996) *School Assemblies – or Collective Worship? Policy Statement.* London, British Humanist Association.

Brown, Alan (1992) *The Multi-faith Church School.* London, National Society.

Brown, Alan (1996) *Between a Rock and a Hard Place: a Report on School Worship.* London, National Society.

Brown, Alan and Brown, Erica (1992) *Primary School Worship.* London, National Society.

Brown, Alan and Furlong, Jean (1996) *Spiritual Development in Schools.* London, National Society.

Brown, Callum (2001) *The Death of Christian Britain.* London, Routledge.

Bruce, S. (1995) *Religion in Modern Britain.* Oxford, Oxford University Press.

Bryan, R. (1997) *Compulsory School Worship: What Do the Pupils Think?* Hull, Martin House.

Burn, J. and Hart, C. (1988) *The Crisis in Religious Education.* Harrow, Educational Research Trust.

Byrne, P. (1995) *Prolegomena to Religious Pluralism: Reference and Realism in Religion.* Basingstoke, Macmillan.

Carey, George et al. (1998) *A Christian Voice in Education: Distinctiveness in Church Schools.* London, National Society and Church House Publishing.

Catholic Education Service (1995) *Spiritual and Moral Development Across the Curriculum. A Discussion Paper for The Professional Development of Teachers in Catholic Schools.* London, CES.

Chadwick, Priscilla (1997) *Shifting Alliances: Church and State in English Education.* London and Washington, Cassell.

Cheetham, Richard (1999) 'The nature and status of religious belief in contemporary Britain, with particular reference to the concept of "truth", as reflected by acts of collective worship in a sample of [town] schools since the 1988 Education Reform Act'. Unpublished PhD thesis, King's College, London.

Christian Action Research and Education (1995) *Policy Statement on Religious Education and Collective Worship*. London, CARE.

Christian Education Movement (1996) *Sensitivity and Awareness: A Guide to Inter-faith Relationships in Schools*. Derby, CEM.

Churches' Joint Education Policy Committee (1995) *Collective Worship in Schools*. London, CJEPC.

Clarke, Peter B. and Byrne, Peter (1993) *Religion Defined and Explained*. Basingstoke, Macmillan.

Cockin, F. A. (1968) 'Worship.' *Learning for Living* 7.4, pp. 7–11.

Cole, W. Owen (ed.) (1983) *Religion in the Multifaith School*. Amersham, Hulton Educational.

Connor, Steven (1989) *Postmodernist Culture: An Introduction to Theories of the Contemporary*. Oxford, Blackwell.

Cooling, T. (1990) 'Science and Religious Education – Conflict or Co-operation?' *British Journal of Religious Education* 13.1, pp. 35–42.

Cooling, T. (1994) *A Christian Vision for State Education*. London, SPCK.

Copley, T. (1989a) *Worship: Worries and Winners*. London, National Society and Church House Publishing.

Copley, T. (1989b) 'The School Community'. *R.E. Today* 6.3, p. 3.

Copley, T. (1997) *Teaching Religion: Fifty years of Religious Education in England and Wales*. Exeter, University of Exeter Press.

Copley, T. (2000) *Spiritual Development in the State School*. Exeter, University of Exeter Press.

Cox, E. (1983) *Problems and Possibilities for Religious Education*. London, Hodder and Stoughton.

Cox, E. and Cairns, Josephine M. (1989) *Reforming Religious Education*. London, Kogan Page.

Culham College Institute (1989) *Christianity in R.E. Programme News*. September 1989. Abingdon, Culham College Institute.

Culham College Institute (1992) *Religious Education and Collective Worship in Primary Schools*. Abingdon, Culham College Institute.

Cupitt, Don (1984) *The Sea of Faith*. London, BBC.

Davie, Grace (1994) *Religion in Britain Since 1945*. Oxford, Blackwell.

Davie, Grace (2000) *Religion in Modern Europe*. Oxford, Oxford University Press.

D'Costa, Gavin (1986) *Theology and Religious Pluralism: the Challenge of Other Religions*. Oxford, Blackwell.

Dent, H. C. (9th edn) (1962) *The Education Act 1944*. London, University of London.

Department for Education (1992) *Choice and Diversity. A new framework for schools*. London, DFE.

Department for Education (1994) *Religious Education and Collective Worship*. Circular 1/94. London, DFE.

Department for Education and Science (1989) *The Education Reform Act 1988: Religious Education and Collective Worship.* Circular 3/89. London, DES.

Doctrine Commission of the Church of England (1976) *Christian Believing.* London, SPCK.

Doctrine Commission of the Church of England (1981) *Believing in the Church.* London, Church House Publishing.

Doctrine Commission of the Church of England (1987) *We Believe in God.* London, Church House Publishing.

Doctrine Commission of the Church of England (1995) *The Mystery of Salvation.* London, Church House Publishing.

Douglas, Bruce (1995) *Thought for the Day.* Leicester, Secondary Heads' Association.

Duncan, Geoffrey (1990) *The Church School.* London, National Society.

Durham Report (1970) *The Fourth R: the Report of the Commission on Religious Education in Schools.* London, National Society and SPCK.

Durkheim, Emile (1915) *The Elementary Forms of the Religious Life.* London, George Allen and Unwin.

Dyer, James and Dony, John (3rd edn) (1975) *The Story of Luton.* Luton, White Crescent Press.

Erricker, Clive (1998) 'Spiritual Confusion: A Critique of current educational policy in England and Wales'. *International Journal of Children's Spirituality* 3.1, pp. 51–63.

European Values Group (1992) *The European Values Study 1981–1990.* London, Gordon Cook Foundation.

Foster, Charles (1961) 'Worship in School'. *Learning for Living* 1.2, pp. 25–7.

Francis, Leslie J. (1987) *Religion in the Primary School.* London, Collins.

Francis, Leslie J. and Kay, William K. (1995) *Teenage Religion and Values.* Leominster, Gracewing Fowler Wright.

Free Church Federal Council (1990) *Collective Worship In County Schools: a Guide to Principles and Practice for Staff, Governors and Other Interested Persons.* London, Free Church Federal Council.

Gellner, Ernest (1991) *Postmodernism, Reason and Religion.* London and New York, Routledge.

General Synod Board of Education and Board of Mission (1991) *All God's Children? Children's Evangelism in Crisis.* London, National Society/Church House Publishing.

Gent, Bill (ed.) (1997) *Assembly Bulletin Autumn Term.* London Borough of Redbridge Education Service.

Gent, W. (1989) *School Worship: Perspectives, Principles and Practice.* Derby, Christian Education Movement.

Giddens, Anthony (ed.) (1972) *Durkheim: Selected Writings.* London, Cambridge University Press.

Gill, R. (1992) *Moral Communities*. Exeter, University of Exeter Press.

Goldman, Ronald (1964) *Religious Thinking from Childhood to Adolescence*. London, Routledge and Kegan Paul.

Gregory, Rachel (1985a) *Assembly*. Ampthill, Bedfordshire Education Service.

Gregory, Rachel (1985b) *Planning Primary R.E.* Ampthill, Bedfordshire Education Service.

Gregory, Rachel (1989) *Collective Worship*. Ampthill, Bedfordshire Education Service.

Grimmit, Michael (1994) 'Religious Education and the Ideology of Pluralism'. *British Journal of Religious Education*. 16.3, pp. 134–42.

Haldane, J. (1990) 'Cultural Pluralism' in Francis, L. and Thatcher, A. (eds) (1990) *Christian Perspectives for Education*. Leominster, Gracewing Fowler Wright, pp. 181–96.

Halman, L. et al. (2001) *The European Values Study: A Third Wave*. Source book of the 1999/2000 European Values Study Surveys. Tilburg, European Values Study.

Halstead, J. Mark (1996) 'Liberal Values and Liberal Education' in Halstead, J. Mark and Taylor, Monica (eds), *Values in Education and Education in Values*. London, Falmer Press.

Halstead, J. M. and Khan-Cheema, A. (1987) 'Muslims and worship in the maintained school'. *Westminster Studies in Education*. Vol. 10, pp. 21–36.

Halstead, J. Mark and Taylor, Monica (eds) (1996) *Values in Education and Education in Values*. London, Falmer Press.

Hardy, Daniel W. (1982) 'Truth in Religious Education: Further Reflections on the Implications of Pluralism' in Hull, J. (ed.) *New Directions in Religious Education*. Lewes, Falmer Press, pp. 109–18.

Hart, Trevor (1995) *Faith Thinking: the Dynamics of Christian Theology*. London, SPCK.

Harte, J. D. C. (1991) 'Worship and Religious Education under the Education Reform Act 1988 – a Lawyer's View'. *British Journal of Religious Education* 13.3, pp. 152–61.

Havel, V. (1996) 'The Search for Meaning in a Global Civilisation' in Anderson, Walter Truett (ed.) *The Fontana Postmodern Reader*. London, Fontana, pp. 208–14.

Havens, T. (1969) 'Encountering our Religious Minorities'. *Learning for Living* 8.3, pp. 31–4.

Hay, D. (1990) *Religious Experience Today: Studying the Facts*. London, Cassell/Mowbray.

Hay, David with Nye, Rebecca (1998) *The Spirit of the Child*. London, HarperCollins.

Hebblethwaite, B. (1988) *The Ocean of Truth: a Defence of Objective Theism*. Cambridge, Cambridge University Press.

Hertfordshire Education Services (1989) *Collective Worship in Hertfordshire: Guidance for Schools, March 1989.* Hertford, Hertfordshire Education Services.

Hertfordshire Education Services (1995) *Collective Worship in Hertfordshire.* Hertford, Hertfordshire Education Services.

Hick, J. (1989) *An Interpretation of Religion: Human Responses to the Transcendent.* London, Macmillan.

Hill, Brian J. (1990) 'Will and Should the Religious Studies Appropriate to Schools in a Pluralistic Society Foster Religious Relativism?' *British Journal of Religious Studies* 12.3, pp. 126–35.

Hirst, Paul H. (1974) *Knowledge and the Curriculum.* London, Routledge and Kegan Paul.

Hirst, Paul H. (1990) 'Christian Education: a contradiction in terms?' in Astley, Jeff and Francis, Leslie J. (eds) *Critical Perspectives on Christian Education.* Leominster, Gracewing Fowler Wright, pp. 305–13.

Hogbin, Jack W. G. (1965) 'The School as a Christian community'. *Learning for Living* 4.3, pp. 21–3.

Hogbin, Jack W. G. (1967) 'Pluralism and Religious Education'. *Learning for Living* 7.1, pp. 21–4.

Holmes, Mark (1992) *Educational Policy for the Pluralist Democracy: the Common School, Choice and Diversity.* Washington DC, London, Falmer Press.

Hope, David (1997) 'A Christian Vision for Education'. Address at conference on the role of Church secondary schools at York, 2 June 1997.

Hughes, J. and Collins, Y. (1996) *Key Stages: Developing Primary School Collective Worship.* London, National Society and Church House Publishing.

Hull, J. (1975) *School Worship: An Obituary.* London, SCM Press.

Hull, J. (1984) *Studies in Religion and Education.* Lewes, Falmer Press.

Hull, J. (1989) *The Act Unpacked.* Birmingham and Isleworth, University of Birmingham and CEM.

Hull, J. (1991) *Mishmash: Religious Education in Multicultural Britain: A Study in Metaphor.* Birmingham and Derby, University of Birmingham and CEM.

Hull, J. (1993) *The Place of Christianity in the Curriculum: the Theology of the Department for Education.* Hockerill Lecture 1993, Hockerill Educational Foundation.

Hull, J. (1995) 'Collective worship: the search for spirituality' in *Future Progress in Religious Education.* Templeton London Lectures, pp. 27–38.

Hulmes, Edward (1979) *Commitment and Neutrality in Religious Education.* London, Chapman.

Hume, Basil (1998) 'Searching for Purpose: God on the Future of our Society'. 15th Arnold Goodman Charity Lecture 28 May 1998.

Inter-Faith Network for the UK (1997) *The Quest for Common Values*. London, The Inter-Faith Network for the UK.

James, W. (1908) *Pragmatism*. London, Longmans, Green.

Jones, C. M. (1969) *Worship in The Secondary School: An Investigation and Discussion*. Oxford, Religious Education Press.

Jowell, R. et al. (eds) (1992) *British Social Attitudes. The Ninth Report. 1992/3*. Social and Community Planning Research. Aldershot, Dartmouth Publishing.

Kant, I. (1929) *Critique of Pure Reason* (translated by Norman Kemp Smith). London, Macmillan.

Kay, William K. (1997) 'Belief in God in Great Britain 1945–1996: Moving the Scenery Behind Classroom R.E.' *British Journal of Religious Education*, 20.1, pp. 28–41.

Kirkham, Richard L. (1995) *Theories of Truth: A Critical Introduction*. Cambridge, Massachusetts, Massachusetts Institute of Technology Press.

Kuhn, Thomas S. (1962) *The Structure of Scientific Revolutions*. Chicago, University of Chicago Press.

Küng, Hans (2000) 'A Global Ethic: A Challenge for the New Millennium'. Gresham Special Lecture, Gresham College, London.

Lewis, C. S. (1943) *The Abolition of Man*. London, Geoffrey Bles.

Lindbeck, George A. (1984) *The Nature of Doctrine*. London, SPCK.

Locke, John (1960) *An Essay concerning Human Understanding* (abridged and edited). London, Fontana/Collins.

Loosemore, A. G. (1965) 'Worship in the County School'. *Theology* LXVIII No. 541, pp. 339–44.

Loukes, Harold (1961) *Teenage Religion*. London, SCM Press.

Luton Education Committee (1997) *Summary of OFSTED Reports (Secondary) 1993–1997. Report of Director of Education*. Luton, Luton Borough Council Education Committee.

Luton Multicultural Education Resources Centre (MERC) (1997) *Focus: Collective Worship. Inset Reference Paper supporting Spiritual & Cultural Development*. Luton, MERC.

McCreery, E. (1993) *Worship in the Primary School*. London, David Fulton.

McGrath, A. E. (1996) *A Passion for Truth: the Intellectual Coherence of Evangelicalism*. Leicester, Apollos.

MacIntyre, A. (1985a) *After Virtue: a Study in Moral Theory*. London, Duckworth.

MacIntyre, A. (1985b) 'Relativism, Power and Philosophy'. *Proceedings and Addresses of the American Philosophical Association*, 59, pp. 5–22.

MacIntyre, A. (1988) *Whose Justice? Which Rationality?* London, Duckworth.

MacIntyre, A. (1994) 'Relativism, Power and Philosophy' in Astley, J. and Francis, Leslie J. (eds) *Critical Perspectives on Christian Education.* Leominster, Gracewing Fowler Wright, pp. 463–83.

McLaughlin, T. (1992) 'Citizenship, Diversity and Education: a Philosophical Perspective'. *Journal of Moral Education,* 21.3, pp. 235–51.

McLaughlin, T. (1995a) 'Liberalism, Education and the Common School'. *Journal of Philosophy of Education,* 29.2, pp. 239–55.

McLaughlin, T. (1995b) 'Public Values, Private Values and Educational Responsibility' in McLaughlin, T. and Pybus, E. (1995) *Values, Education and Responsibility.* St Andrews Centre for Philosophy and Public Affairs, pp. 19–34.

McLeod, H. (1995) 'The Privatization of Religion in Modern England' in Young, Frances (ed.) *Dare We Speak of God in Public?* London, Mowbray, pp. 4–21.

Markham, Ian (1998) *Truth and the Reality of God.* Edinburgh, T. & T. Clark.

Middleton, J. Richard and Walsh, Brian J. (1995) *Truth is Stranger than it Used to Be.* London, SPCK.

Miles, G. (1990) *Managing Collective Worship.* Leicester, Secondary Heads Association.

Miles, Matthew B. and Huberman, A. Michael (1984) *Qualitative Data Analysis: Sourcebook of New Methods.* Beverly Hills, California, Sage Publications.

Mitchell, B. G. (1970) 'Indoctrination' in Durham Report (1970) *The Fourth R.* London, National Society and SPCK, pp. 353–8.

Mitchell, B. G. (1994) 'Faith and Reason: A False Antithesis?' in Astley, J. and Francis, L. J. (eds) *Critical Perspectives on Christian Education.* Leominster, Gracewing Fowler Wright, pp. 345–59.

Mitchell, Peter J. (1997) 'Education, Religion and Transcendental Values'. *Muslim Educational Quarterly* 14.2, pp. 5–15.

Murphy, James (1971) *Church, State and Schools in Britain 1800–1970.* London, Routledge & Kegan Paul.

Muslim Education Forum (1997) *Collective Worship in State Funded Schools.* Birmingham, Muslim Education Forum.

Muslim Educational Trust (1995) *Education in Multi-Faith Britain: Meeting the Needs of Muslims.* London, Muslim Educational Trust.

National Association of Head Teachers (1985) *Religious Education in Schools.* Haywards Heath, NAHT.

National Association of Head Teachers (1994) *Survey of Heads on RE and Collective Worship.* Haywards Heath, NAHT.

National Association of Head Teachers (1995) *Policy Statement on Collective Worship.* Haywards Heath, NAHT.

National Association of SACREs (1995) *Statement on Collective Worship*.

National Forum for Values in Education and the Community (1996) *Consultation on Values in Education and the Community*. London, SCAA.

National Society (1989) *School Worship*. London, National Society.

National Union of Teachers (1989) *The Education Reform Act 1988: Religious Education and Collective Worship. Guidance and Information For Teacher Governors, Headteachers and School Representatives*. London, NUT.

Newbigin, Lesslie (1982) 'Teaching Religion in a Secular Plural Society' in Hull, J. (ed.) *New Directions in Religious Education*. Lewes, Falmer Press, pp. 97–107.

Newbigin, Lesslie (1989) *The Gospel in a Pluralist Society*. London, SPCK.

Newbigin, Lesslie (1990) 'Religion, Science and Truth in the School Curriculum' in Francis, L. and Thatcher, A. (eds) *Christian Perspectives for Education*. Leominster, Gracewing Fowler Wright, pp. 93–9.

Newsom Report (1963) *Half Our Future: a Report of the Central Advisory Council for Education (England)*. London, HMSO.

Nipkow, Karl Ernst (1993) 'Oikumene – the Global Horizon for Christian and Religious Education'. *British Journal of Religious Education*. 15.2, pp. 5–11.

Ofsted (1994a) *Religious Education and Collective Worship 1992–1993*. London, HMSO.

Ofsted (1994b) *Spiritual, Moral, Social and Cultural Development: an OFSTED Discussion Paper*. London, Ofsted.

Ofsted (1995a) *Religious Education: a Review of Inspection Findings 1993/94*. London, HMSO.

Ofsted (1995b) *The OFSTED Handbook: Guidance on the Inspection of Nursery and Primary Schools*. London, HMSO.

Ofsted (1995c) *The OFSTED Handbook: Guidance on the Inspection of Secondary Schools*. London, HMSO.

Ofsted (1997) *Standards and Quality in Education – Annual Report HMCI 1995–1996*. London, Ofsted.

Ofsted (1998a) *Secondary Education 1993–1997: a Review of Secondary Schools in England*. London, HMSO.

Ofsted (1998b) *Standards in Primary Religious Education*. London, Ofsted.

O'Leary, Joseph Stephen (1996) *Religious Pluralism and Christian Truth*. Edinburgh, Edinburgh University Press.

Orchard, Stephen (1992) *The Pursuit of Truth in Community: a Christian View of Education*. Derby, CEM.

Osborn, L. (1995) *Restoring the Vision: the Gospel and Modern Culture*. London, Mowbray.

Pailin, David (1986) *Groundwork of Philosophy of Religion*. London, Epworth Press.

Parsons, Marion (1995) *Managing Policies*. Kingswood, Bristol, Secondary Heads Association.

Phillips, D. Z. (1968) 'Philosophy and Religious Education' in Astley, J. and Francis, Leslie (eds) (1994) *Critical Perspectives on Christian Education*. Leominster, Gracewing Fowler Wright, pp. 439–52.

Phillips Griffiths, A. (ed.) (1967) *Knowledge and Belief*. London, Oxford University Press.

Plowden Report (1967) *Children and Their Primary Schools*. London, HMSO.

Polanyi, Michael (1958) *Personal Knowledge*. London, Routledge and Kegan Paul.

Prescott, D. M. (ed.) (1953) *Junior Teacher's Assembly Book*. Poole, Blandford Press.

Priestley, J. G. (1996) *Spirituality in the Curriculum*. Hockerill Lecture 1996. King's College, London.

Race, Alan (2nd edn) (1993) *Christians and Religious Pluralism*. London, SCM Press.

R.E. Council in England and Wales (1996) *Collective Worship in Schools*. Oxford, Culham Educational Foundation.

R.E. Council in England and Wales, the National Association of SACREs, the Interfaith Network for the UK (1998) *Collective Worship Reviewed: Report of the 1997 Consultation*. Abingdon, Culham College Institute.

Robinson, John A. T. (1963) *Honest to God*. London, SCM Press.

Robson, Geoff (1996) 'Religious Education, Government Policy and Professional Practice 1985–1995'. *British Journal of Religious Education* 19.1, pp. 13–23.

Roger, A. R. (1982) *Education and Faith in an Open Society*. Edinburgh, Handsel Press.

Rudge, Linda (1998) 'I am Nothing – Does It Matter? A Critique of Current Religious Education Policy and Practice in England on behalf of the Silent Majority'. *British Journal of Religious Education* 20.3, pp. 155–65.

Runzo, Joseph (1986) *Reason, Relativism and God*. Basingstoke, Macmillan.

Sacks, J. (1991) *The Persistence of Faith*. London, Weidenfeld and Nicolson.

Sacks, J. (1995) *Faith in the Future*. London, Darton, Longman and Todd.

Sacks, J. (1997) *The Politics of Hope*. London, Jonathan Cape.

Sarwar, Ghulam (1989) *The Education Reform Act 1988: What Can Muslims Do?* London, Muslim Educational Trust.

Sarwar, Ghulam (revised edition) (1994) *British Muslims and Schools.* London, Muslim Educational Trust.

Schmitt, Frederick F. (1995) *Truth: a Primer.* Oxford, Westview Press.

School Curriculum and Assessment Authority (1995a) *Spiritual and Moral Development.* SCAA Discussion Paper No. 3. London, SCAA Publications.

School Curriculum and Assessment Authority (1995b) *Analysis of SACRE Reports 1995.* London, SCAA Publications.

School Curriculum and Assessment Authority (1996a) *Education for Adult Life: the Spiritual and Moral Development of Young People.* SCAA Discussion Paper No. 6. London, SCAA Publications.

School Curriculum and Assessment Authority (1996b) *Analysis of SACRE Reports 1996.* London, SCAA Publications.

School Curriculum and Assessment Authority (1997) *Analysis of SACRE Reports 1997.* London, SCAA Publications.

Schools Council (1971) *Religious Education in Secondary Schools.* Working Paper no. 36. London, Evans/Methuen Educational.

Schools Council (1972) *Religious Education in Primary Schools.* Working Paper no. 44. London, Evans/Methuen Educational.

Sealey, John (1985) *Religious Education: Philosophical Perspectives.* London, George Allen and Unwin.

Second Vatican Ecumenical Council (1966) *Declaration on the Relation of the Church to non-Christian religions.* London, Catholic Truth Society.

Shepherd, P. (1998) *Values for Church Schools.* London, National Society and Church House Publishing.

Shortt, John and Cooling, Trevor (eds) (1997) *Agenda for Educational Change.* Leicester, Apollos.

Skeie, Geir (1995) 'Plurality and Pluralism: a Challenge for Religious Education'. *British Journal of Religious Education* 17.2, pp. 84–91.

Smart, Ninian (1969) *The Religious Experience of Mankind.* Glasgow, Collins.

Smith, David (1997) 'Facing the Challenge of Educational Change' in Shortt, J. and Cooling, T. (eds) *Agenda for Educational Change.* Leicester, Apollos, pp. 24–38.

Snook, I. A. (1972) *Indoctrination and Education.* London, Routledge and Kegan Paul.

Soskice, Janet Martin (1992) 'The Truth Looks Different from Here'. *New Blackfriars*, 73, pp. 528–41

Souper, P. and Kay, W. (1983) *The School Assembly Debate: 1942–1982.* Southampton, University of Southampton, Department of Education.

Suffolk County Council Education Department (1995) *Towards Realism and Consensus: Guidelines for Collective Worship in a Plural Society.* Suffolk County Council.

Swann Report (1985) *Education for All.* London, HMSO.

Tate, N. (1996) *Education for Adult Life.* Speech at SCAA conference, 15 January 1996.

Tate, N. (1998) *What is Education for? The Fifth Annual Education Lecture.* School of Education, King's College, London.

Taylor, Monica J. (1998) *Values Education and Values in Education.* London, ATL.

Thatcher, Adrian (1999) *Spirituality and the Curriculum.* London, Cassell.

Thiessen, Elmer John (1993) *Teaching for Commitment.* Leominster, Gracewing and Montreal, McGill-Queen's University Press.

Usher, Robin and Edwards, Richard (1994) *Postmodernism and Education: Different Voices, Different Worlds.* London, Routledge.

Vroom, Hendrik M. (1989) *Religions and the Truth: Philosophical Reflections and Perspectives.* Grand Rapids, Michigan, Wm. B. Eerdmans.

Wakeman, Brian (1995) 'My Way – Brian Wakeman Tells How he Teaches'. *Times Educational Supplement* 4136, 6 October 1995.

Warnock, Mary (1996) 'Moral Values' in Halstead, J. Mark and Taylor, M.J. *Values in Education and Education in Values.* London, Falmer Press, pp. 45–53.

Watson, Brenda (1987) *Education and Belief.* Oxford, Blackwell.

Webster, D. (1990) 'School Worship'. *British Journal of Religious Education* 12.3, pp. 151–9.

Webster, D. (1995) *Collective Worship in Schools.* Cleethorpes, Kenelm Press.

White, Alan R. (1970) *Truth.* London, Macmillan.

Wiles, Maurice (1992) *Christian Theology and Inter-Religious Dialogue.* London, SCM Press.

Wilson, B. (1966) *Religion in Secular Society.* Harmondsworth, Pelican.

Wolffe, John (1993) 'The Religions of the Silent Majority' in Parsons, Gerald (ed.) *The Growth of Religious Diversity: Britain from 1945, Vol. 1: Traditions.* London, Routledge in association with The Open University, pp. 305–46.

Woodhead, L. and Heelas, P. (2000) *Religion in Modern Times.* Oxford, Blackwell.

Woozley, A. D. (1949) *Theory of Knowledge: An Introduction.* London, Hutchinson.

Wright, Andrew (1993) *Religious Education in the Secondary School.* London, David Fulton.

Wright, Andrew (1998) *Religious Education, Religious Literacy, and Democratic Citizenship*. Unpublished paper.

Wright, Andrew (2000) *Spirituality and Education*. London, Routledge Falmer.

Young, David (1994) *Collective Worship: an Address to the National Association of SACREs* on 10 December 1994.

Young, Frances (ed.) (1995) *Dare We Speak of God in Public?* London, Mowbray.

Index

UNIVERSITY OF WALES, NEWPORT
LIBRARY AND INFORMATION SERVICES CAERLEON